GRINGA
LATINA

GRINGA

A WOMAN OF

TWO WORLDS

LATINA

Houghton Mifflin Company

BOSTON   NEW YORK

1995

LATINA

TWO WORLDS

A WOMAN OF

GRINGA

Gabriella De Ferrari

AUTHOR'S NOTE: This is a nonfiction book of reconstructed memories. Given the subjectivity of memory, I may have inadvertently altered some of the names of the people and places in this story. I have deliberately changed others, in order to protect the privacy of my family and friends.

A special thank-you to Lynn Nesbit, Karen Durbin, and Sally Ganz. Also, gratitude to Gail Winston and John Sterling.

For information about permission to reproduce selections from this book, write to Permissions, Houghton Mifflin Company, 215 Park Avenue South, New York, New York 10003.

Library of Congress Cataloging-in-Publication Data

De Ferrari, Gabriella.
    Gringa Latina : a woman of two worlds / Gabriella De Ferrari.
    p. cm.
  ISBN 0-395-70934-2
1. De Ferrari, Gabriella — Homes and haunts — Peru.   2. Women novel- ists, American — 20th century — Biography.   3. De Ferrari, Garbriella — Childhood and youth.   4. Italians — Peru — Social life and customs.   5. Peruvian Americans — Biography.   6. Italian Americans — Biography.   I. Title.
PS3554.E1115Z468   1995
813'.54 — dc20   94-24138   [B]   CIP

Book design by Anne Chalmers

Printed in the United States of America

QUM 10 9 8 7 6 5 4 3 2 1

"Haven't you ever thought, you gringoes,
that all this land was once ours?"

— from *The Old Gringo*,
by Carlos Fuentes

*G*RINGA
LATINA

PROLOGUE

Gringa Latina is a celebration of my growing up as a gringa in a land of Latinos and becoming a Latina in a land of gringos. I was a gringa in Peru, because my parents had come from a distant land to make their life there; I have been called a Latina in Saint Louis, Boston, Los Angeles, and New York, the places where I have made my life as an adult. Yet I am not one or the other but both. Like mirrors, they are the reflection of each other, their images continually resonating throughout my life. These reflections, with their peaceful islands and their turbulent waters, form the chapters of this book. Not everything here is my life as it happened, yet the book is my truth, with its fragile edges filtered through the veils of passion and time, shaped as it made its way into these pages. This is the fiction of memory.

I grew up in a land of cloudless skies, in a rainless valley rendered fertile by an almost dry river, breathing air sparkled with silt. The only clouds I remember were those made by the desert sand, which rose behind our car as we drove to the beach each Sunday. Like brown sails, they formed and vanished into the vastness. The clouds followed us as we made the long drive from immense dryness to immense wetness. My parents sat in the front seat talking with each other in Italian, the language that we spoke as a family. My sister, brother, and I sat in the back, our lives bound together on parallel courses in a country so mysterious.

We grew up in a world of extremes: too much of some things and nothing at all of others. Peru, the country of my past, was a place where silent condors topped the silent Andes, where the enormous waves of the Pacific continually raped the arid desert, never able to turn it fertile, where groceries arrived at the markets on the backs of llamas and mules, and where hungry country priests melted down their silver altars and sold them for food. In this place, where hope often turned into despair, my parents set down their roots and I planted my own.

Though I call myself Peruvian, I am not that alone. My roots are also in other, more distant places. We in our family were taller and whiter than our neighbors; some of us even had blond hair. We brought customs with us that stuck, like having a house at the beach — a house made of wood, which stood perched on the rocks like a nest for some odd, large bird that wanted her eggs to hatch in a place surrounded by sand and sky and water.

My parents came to Peru as adults, my father looking for adventure and freedom, my mother following her adoration of him. They both learned to love Peru, and its strong identity became their own. My father's was an instant love affair; my mother's took a long time to develop. At first she appreciated this place only because her husband did, but toward the end of her life, she developed a fierce attachment to Peru and chose to die there.

Peru marks the first fifteen years of my life, and it informs all my lives that have come afterward. Now, living in America, I am often asked how this feels. In answering this question for myself, for my children, for my friends, and even for strangers, I have drawn my own map of Peru. That map has become this book, saturated with powerful echoes and profound longings for a place I can never leave behind.

My own Peru is filled with the things that I wanted to stay the same and that have: the purple-tinted light as it filters through the blooming jacarandas; the taste of my favorite dish, papa a la huancaina, made of hot peppers and lush potatoes; the gentle rhythms of the kind of Spanish that is spoken there. My memory is also filled with things that have changed which I wish had not: the calmness of growing up in Tacna, then a small town; the slow harmonies of the lives of the people that populated my childhood; the absence of terrorism and drug traffic. Then there are the changes I am happy to see: the jets that cross the skies, the huge roads that cut across the Andes, the young women struggling to break away from the narrow traditions that once kept them from having professional lives.

There are also the many enigmas of Peru, such as the gigantic Nazca lines, drawn deep in the desert by people generations ago. Did they hope to take themselves closer to God? And how was it possible that the might of the Inca civilization was destroyed by a handful of Spaniards? Above all, there is the tragic mystery of why the country's riches sit idle, failing to provide a decent life for its people.

Still, for me Peru is a refuge, a place I long to return to in moments of despair and homesickness. I imagine myself arriving in the safe womb of the small plane of my youth to find my parents at the bottom of the steps, waiting to take me home to my scents and my textures.

This is the Peru that resides in my interior rhythms as I make my way in crowded New York, as I prepare ceviche or speak Spanish with my children. All these territories coalesce and reside in my emotional and intellectual landscape, "Peru-familiar," like the sweet scent of the dust clouds of my childhood, mysterious like the life of the desert. I think about the intensity of this emotional territory, of the secret languages, of the many years of silent internal debate before finally realizing that Peru is where the important parts of myself belong.

1

OUR PERUVIAN FRIEND

SEÑORITA LUISA was my mother's best friend. Together they made an odd pair — two women, two continents. Señorita Luisa's internal music was based on the five notes of the ancient melancholic melodies of the Andes, while Mother's was based on the seven notes of her European scales. Señorita Luisa moved at a slow, even pace, as if she carried the burdens of her ancestors, a people with a glorious past and a troubled, uncertain present. She had the blood of the Indians to whom the country belonged, mixed with that of its conquerors, the Spaniards, who robbed Peru of its indigenous culture and so much else. Mother's movements were fast and constantly changing. Like a boat sailing in new waters, Mother was searching for her place. Her family as far back as it could be traced was Italian, and like so many Italians who emigrated, she carried with her a fearless sense of adventure. To her, everything was new and exciting, yet hard to accept. Mother was tall and fair, and her very blue eyes danced as if echoing her gestures and movements. Señorita Luisa was a short, stocky woman who always dressed in black. Her features were sharp, as if they had been chiseled of stone. Her skin was olive-toned, and deep crevices cut across her forehead. She talked in long, slow sentences and often interrupted them with sighs that seemed to come from a very deep part of her, as if from the bottom of a black pond. Though she and my mother were the same age, she always seemed old to me. In contrast, Mother always seemed to me young — and transparent, like a crystal lake.

Our parents taught us to pay strict attention to everything Señorita Luisa said. She was our dictionary of Peruvianisms. I assumed that just as everything about us seemed strange to most Peruvians, everything about her was typical of the other locals.

Señorita Luisa came from one of those families that populate the literature of South American countries and have earned our writers the name of magic realists. Their stories are filled with the illegitimate children of priests, old maids' daughters locked in convents, triplets born attached, saints who appear with fiancées, ghosts that surface in the silence of the night to be consulted about family matters, old men who ride into the night to rape young girls in order to prove their masculinity. Señorita Luisa's family history was filled with such episodes, including the enigmatic and wholesale deaths of her brothers.

She was always treated as a reject because she had never married, a status that caused paralyzing fear in every Peruvian female. Women in the Peru of my childhood were completely dependent on men. From birth, girls were taught to pray for a husband, and the wedding day marked a woman's ultimate achievement in life. The search for a husband was an elaborate, ritualized hunt regulated by strict rules. Poor Señorita Luisa had broken the most serious of these. She had been deserted by her suitor, who left to marry someone else. It was not as if she had done anything wrong herself, yet once abandoned, she became totally undesirable. Having been engaged meant that you were not ever to be considered by another man. Mother told us that it was very sad. My friends at school spoke about it in hushed tones, as a great horrible curse.

So Señorita Luisa stayed at home and obeyed her parents, to whom she knew she was an embarrassment. When her mother got too tired or too lazy to run the house, Señorita Luisa took over. Her trousseau trunk was put away. She cut her hair short, stopped wearing lipstick, and thereafter dressed in black.

Señorita Luisa's father had been a business associate of my father's. He was a rich landowner who lived to see all five of his sons die of an undiagnosed illness within a year. At the end of his life he went to Father and asked him to look after his daughter. And that was how she came into our lives.

Our maid Saturnina, who would tell me the grown-ups' secrets, explained that at first Mother did not want to hear of this friendship. She assumed that Señorita Luisa was an old girlfriend of Father's, but when she met her, Señorita Luisa's loneliness went right through her. After asking Father for forgiveness, Mother took her on. Señorita Luisa became an intimate friend, almost part of the family, and moved to a house across the street.

Saturnina also told me that all the brothers' deaths had been caused by a curse put on the family by the souls of the people who had worked on their plantation and been treated badly. At home we were taught to believe in tragedies, not curses. I never could tell the difference, but I taught myself to call them tragedies at home and curses everywhere else.

Crossing the street from my house to the home of Señorita Luisa was like crossing a continent, so different were the worlds in which we lived. Whereas everything in my house was orderly and rational, everything in hers was chaotic and confusing. In our house every room had a specific function; in hers, except for the

kitchen, all the rooms served all purposes. Our furniture was always in the same place; hers was constantly
rearranged. Mother knew precisely where everything
was; Señorita Luisa could never find anything. Her
drawers were like bottomless treasure chests from which
the strangest things emerged: cooking spices in her
bedroom drawers, cinnamon-scented perfume in the
kitchen. Her bathroom, like most people's, was outside
the house, in a little building all its own. As a child, I
never thought that our house was more modern. I
always assumed that we were simply different for specific reasons, and when my friends came to visit I was
embarrassed by ordinary things, such as our indoor
bathroom or the fact that our car was kept in something called a garage.

At mealtimes, not only did Señorita Luisa's entire
house smell of food, but the scent spread into the
garden and the street; in our house, great efforts were
made to contain food odors in the kitchen. Her servants were fed servant food; ours ate what we did. The
trees in her garden looked exhausted, as if the leaves
had fought the weight of the desert dust to be born;
our trees, which my parents had imported from Italy,
were young and green, their lacy leaves shimmering in
the light. Our garden was arranged in neat rows with
the colors of the flowers and the shades of the greens
graduated to make a harmonious whole, while hers was
a tangle of jasmine next to mint next to sprawling

cucumbers. One had to climb over tall bushes to reach the fruit trees, yet everything in her garden was bigger and smelled sweeter, including the fruits that grew hidden under cobwebs.

One of my earliest memories is the scent of Señorita Luisa's house on an evening when I was asked not to go to bed but to accompany my parents on a condolence call. The smell was heavy, airless, as if candles had been burning and wet mud had been mixed with the fragrance of lilies — the kind of scent that makes it hard to find air for the next breath. I was dressed in my fancy clothes, stiff with starch, and I felt uncomfortable. We followed a maid down an endlessly long hallway with a tall ceiling that was occasionally interrupted by a dusty skylight, which brought in a shy evening light. We walked hesitantly, aware of the echoes in the emptiness. It was my first formal visit. I had been told exactly how to behave and what to say.

Señorita Luisa was sitting at the end of the very large living room, which was dark and filled with people who stood as silent as the furniture. She was dressed all in black, and a veil hid her face. A ghost, I thought to myself, and I forgot the lines I was supposed to say. She reached for me and gave me a tender hug. She didn't have her usual cinnamon smell but exuded a sort of piercing aroma, like the scent of Mother's trunks from Italy. My parents and I made our way to a corner by a window. We sat and waited in a silence that was interrupted only by Señorita Luisa's deep sighs. They made my heart feel small and empty. We were there because her father, who had been her only living relative, had died.

It was my first encounter with death. My parents told me that it is a long sleep that comes after a tiring life, but the next day, when I was left alone with Señorita Luisa, I was told something different. Death, she said, is when the Lord calls you and you go to be with Him. It is what you live for. If you are good and live for Him, you go to inhabit His kingdom filled with angels and happiness. If you are bad, you go to live with the devils in a very hot place called hell. However, if you do some bad things, repent, and confess, you go to purgatory, and your friends' and families' prayers can get you out. A Hail Mary spares you six years, and a whole rosary one hundred. Every sin had a price in terms of years in purgatory and number of prayers for redemption. Masses bought you centuries, which Señorita Luisa informed me were nothing compared to eternity. She made me pray with her. I assumed her father had been very bad, because she was planning to have so many masses said for him. Mother told me it was just a story that priests tell to keep people going to church.

Señorita Luisa also possessed an army of saints to whom she prayed for various favors. When I lost something concrete, she taught me to pray to Saint Anthony; when I lost my patience, Santa Rita could help me recover it. Mother also thought this was nonsense. Early in life I realized that there were two very different ways of looking at the world, my parents' and Señorita Luisa's. What she told me was what I assumed the world outside my house believed, and what I was told at home was what people believed in that faraway place where my parents came from. I kept them separate and functioned accordingly, never suffering from the difference, at least while I was young and the lines were so easy to draw. Yet Señorita Luisa's world, together with that of the maids in the kitchen, was far more seductive than the rational world of my parents. I liked curses, and miracles, and praying for a handsome husband, and buying up heaven.

Mother and Señorita Luisa talked to each other constantly. They would sit under a large mulberry tree in the afternoon and become absorbed in each other's stories. My own time with Señorita Luisa came in the evenings, when I got back from school. I would go to her house for a snack of hot chocolate and a cake she made especially for me of fresh figs held together with what she called "honey glue." She had many stories to tell, and they were all equally outrageous. I listened, mesmerized by her tales, delivered in the monotonous rhythms of her voice as if they occurred every day, like drinking milk or taking a bath.

My favorite stories were about her brothers. When she talked about them, her eyes filled with tears and her voice grew low. One had to speak softly about the dead out of respect for them. I had to sit close so I wouldn't miss anything. Her brothers, she told me, had been handsome and brave and had lived lives of danger and adventure. They were one year apart in age and had died when the oldest was twenty-two. They had never gone to school but had been tutored in their hacienda, and had learned to write and read and do math.

They had also been instructed in the difficult tasks of running their huge landholding. The family had been granted the land, a fertile swath by a river in the otherwise dry desert, many generations before. At the time that Señorita Luisa's brothers were alive, her family did not have a house in town; they lived on the plantation, which was two hours away by car. They grew olives and cotton — fields and fields of white pima cotton, the most desirable for the export market, sold in distant places like England and France. The olives were picked and packed in huge barrels and sent to Spain to be made into oil.

The plantation was completely self-sustaining. It had its own vegetable garden, animals for meat and milk, vineyards to make wine, and many *peones*, the Indians who came from the mountains to work. Señorita Luisa's brothers got up at dawn and traveled around the plantation on horseback, making sure the men did their work. They parceled out the water from the river so there was enough for all the crops. The women servants took their lunch to the fields. The main meal, however, was served early in the evening, when they came back covered with dust and sweat. "We made everything," Señorita Luisa told me with great pride, "sausages, cakes, and jams, even chocolates and candies." The kitchen alone employed twelve women. I imagined it to be some kind of factory. When I finally visited it, I was disappointed to see how primitive it was. The stoves were heated by coal. The kitchen was black and airless, there was a heavy smell of oil, and flies were everywhere.

After dinner, Señorita Luisa's brothers had played the guitar, and later, before going to bed, they had worked on the accounts. On Sunday the four youngest rode off to the plantation next to theirs, a three-hour ride, to visit their girlfriends — four sisters, pale, beautiful, always dressed in pastel organdy dresses. Each of the girls was named after a river. Rivers brought fertility, and their father, who had never had a son, wanted many grandchildren. Their river names were odd: Ucayali, Caplina, Amazona, and Rimac. Señorita Luisa reassured me that each also had the Christian name Maria, like the Virgin. Most Peruvian girls had two names, and one was almost always Maria.

Later, when the brothers went to the capital, they brought each of the sisters a ring of emeralds and diamonds. It was hard to get Señorita Luisa to talk about romantic love. I never brought it up, because I had been warned by Saturnina never to discuss that subject with old maids; it made them too sad. Señorita Luisa told me that her brothers' interest in the sisters was "real love, not arranged love, or love of convenience." They were all to be married. When the brothers died, the sisters went to a convent and never came out. Señorita Luisa went to visit them, but they wouldn't receive her because they couldn't bear the grief.

Señorita Luisa's brother Jacinto, the oldest, had no girlfriend; he had a "woman," an Indian woman whom he loved. She lived on the plantation, and their love affair was a secret one. When he died, she committed suicide; she was pregnant with his child. When Señorita Luisa got to this part of the story, we both cried. "Just imagine," she would say, "I could have brought up that child."

I can still see the picture of her brothers that she kept by the side of her bed: five short, stocky young men with wide mustaches and large Panama hats, standing next to tall white horses. I so much wanted to have a boyfriend who looked like one of them.

Señorita Luisa also told me stories about the Indians and the Spaniards. From her I learned what the Spaniards had done to my country. Her views were different from what we were taught at school, where the nuns called Spain "the mother country" and said it had brought Catholicism and civilization to the "unfortunate" native creatures. Señorita Luisa believed that the

Spaniards had ruined a civilization, doped the Indians with coca, and made them slave in the silver and gold mines for the benefit of Spain's greedy queen.

Señorita Luisa didn't even like Columbus, a hero of mine. I thought it wonderful that he had been so brave, as brave as my father, who had come so far to look for adventure. But I never dared to disagree with Señorita Luisa. I feared that if I did, she would stop telling me stories; children were supposed to respect adults and not question their judgment. It seemed strange that she felt that way about the Spaniards. Saturnina and the maids in the kitchen talked about them with such respect: *conquistadores*, they called them.

One of my favorite activities, in which Señorita Luisa would indulge me only when she was in a good mood, was to have my fortune read. She would drip hot wax from a candle into a large container of icy water. When the wax hit the water, it formed different shapes. She read them and told me my "little future," that is, my future for the next week. The prognostications were mostly designed to teach me to behave: "This week you will tell a lie and that will cost you, because your mother will not believe you anymore," or "You never finish your prayers at Mass, and tomorrow the devil is going to pull your leg." Only occasionally would she tell me my "big future," the one I wanted to hear the most: a handsome man would fall in love with me, a man with green eyes and dark hair like her brothers.

The maids in my family's kitchen were also constantly reading wax, but they weren't allowed to do it for me. My mother thought it was nonsense. She never knew that Señorita Luisa read my fortune. Señorita Luisa also told ghost stories about the *almas*, the souls of the dead that came to visit at night. She used to scare me so much I had to ask Saturnina to stay with me until I fell asleep. Saturnina knew how to send the souls away: she tied a black ribbon to the window and left them a piece of bread.

As Señorita Luisa had saints, Saturnina and the other maids had roots and herbs. These could perform any kind of miracle, especially scaring away the evil eye that women gave each other when they were interested in the same man. I was constantly torn between wanting to believe Señorita Luisa and Saturnina and wanting to believe Mother, who was more interested in having me worry about geography and math.

Over the years, on my trips back to Peru, I would visit Señorita Luisa. She never changed much, but got smaller and sadder and developed a greater vocabulary of saints to pray to. "Everyone I loved died before me," she often told me. "Their souls keep me company, but they haven't yet given me the gift of calling me to be with them."

As I think about her life, doomed to be lonely because a man once scorned her, I wonder what she thought about mine, my career, my divorces. She found a way to explain me to herself. "Your family, you are gringos, *extranjeros*. I was never able to teach your mother to be one of us. She wanted to, and in some ways she was. But then she sent you away. I told her not to do it, that she would lose you. And she did. You stayed away. Don't forget your country, though," she always added. "It is a great country."

Señorita Luisa often spoke about Father, and when she did, her eyes filled with tears. "I remember your father," she would say, "probably better than you do. You were so young when he died. He was one of us. But then, it is easier for a man. A man's world, the world of business, is the same everywhere."

The last time I saw Señorita Luisa, shortly before she died, she asked many questions that must have been on her mind for a long time. She wanted to know if Americans were religious people, if my children had been baptized, if the pope had annulled my marriages. I answered yes on all counts, knowing that sometimes it's better not to tell the truth.

2

SATURNINA

SATURNINA CAME from a small village in the Andes called Tarata, a village so poor there was no electricity, no running water, not even a paved road to reach it. She was one of the thousands of Indian girls who came to the cities to find jobs as household help. In Peru at that time even the most modest of families employed a maid. The Indian women came to find "the promised land"; instead they found frustrated housewives who exploited them.

Maids came and went in my house, but Saturnina stayed with my family for a long time, becoming a friend and an ally. She was seventeen when she arrived, full of life, and anxious to work and be loyal. She had the olive complexion and the high cheekbones typical of Indian women. Her long black hair, which matched the color of her eyes, was held together in two braids. Her mouth was like a tiny dot in her face, but it opened up into a wide, contagious smile. She spoke good Spanish and had an odd habit of covering her face with her hands when asked to do something she felt unable to do. "Teach me, *patrona*," she would beg. There was nothing she was not willing to try.

Unlike the other maids, who were inscrutable, Saturnina had an open disposition and loved to talk. We were only eight years apart when she came to our house. She was the maid assigned to the children, so she spent a lot of time with us instead of in the kitchen, where the others congregated. Her life story was similar to that of many of the other maids, except that most of them came to us directly from the sierra, while Saturnina had worked for another family before us.

Saturnina did not know who her father was. By the time she was old enough to remember, her mother was living with another man. Her mother had nine children by five or six different men, but only three of them survived childhood. Saturnina's earliest recollections were of her mother being beaten by the man she lived with, who often arrived drunk at night. "I can't understand it, Niña Gabriella," she said. "I think Indian women like being beaten. My mother used to say, 'He loves me, he beats me.'"

Her family lived in a one-room house where everyone ate, slept, and cooked. They had only one bed, in which her mother and her mother's lover slept. At ten, Saturnina was raped by her mother's lover. "When I told my mother, she said that I had to get used to it, because men were like that. I was so afraid of him that one day I ran away and came to Tacna. In the marketplace I met a woman who said I could work for her. She said she couldn't pay me, but she would give me a roof to live under and food to eat. She also told me she would give me a day off every week and allow me to go to school in the evenings.

"The woman lived in a large house. Her husband was an army captain, and they had three sons, who were little and unruly. When I arrived at her house, she bathed me and washed my hair in something called DDT. We Indians knew no hygiene and carried with us bugs that gave white people strange diseases. I didn't mind being made clean, but it hurt and burned so much. She also threw away my clothes and gave me a uniform to wear. She taught me to cook, to clean, to do the wash, and to iron. I don't think they had a lot of money, because I was the only maid. I worked from morning until night, never went to school, and never got the day off I was promised.

"But my *patrona* was kind. I knew no Spanish, and she helped me learn the language. She let me listen to the *radio-novela* with her. I went with her to the market every day. On the way I used to pass by your house, so big, with all those green plants and flowers. I knew I wanted to work here someday. I stayed with that family for a long time. I was not happy or unhappy. There was so much new and special in that house, especially the food we ate. In my village we ate only potatoes and corn, and on special occasions, llama meat. In the *patrona*'s house I had my own bed, and a light at night, and a shower to make myself clean. She taught me to knit, and I made myself a sweater to wear on Sundays.

My mother found out where I was and came to get me. My *patrona* gave her money, and my mother let me stay.

"One night my two little *patrones* came to my room. They were naked and got into my bed. They wanted me to do things I didn't want to do, as my mother's lover had. I screamed. Their father came and ordered the boys to leave. The next day the *patrona* told me I had to go. I was very sad. I was very afraid. I had no money. I went to the market and asked a woman who sold fish to ask your mother if she needed a maid. That is how I came to this house."

What Saturnina wanted most was to learn to read and write. She went to school in the evenings, but she was smart and didn't feel she was learning fast enough. She borrowed my schoolbooks and sat with us when we did our homework. Soon she was doing math and picking up Italian words. She was the only maid we ever had who learned to speak Italian.

Saturnina also wanted to learn to be a "real Catholic." She told me that in the sierra, the priests were the worst men. She told me that they raped women and made them steal food from their homes. They got everything they wanted by threatening people with hell. Like most Indians, Saturnina followed a religion that was a mixture of the Catholicism forced on the people by the Spaniards and their own traditions. Although she believed in saints and miracles, she also believed in omens and curses and was deathly afraid of

Mother Earth, who could bring winds that would kill plants and animals.

On Sundays, Saturnina would put on her best dress (a simple yellow cotton print with tiny daisies), tie a bright ribbon to the bottom of her braids, and head with the other maids for the plaza, where their social life took place. What happened then she never told us, and Mother said not to ask, but it became clear that there was a direct relationship between Sundays off and the fact that so many maids ended up pregnant. Saturnina looked down on the maids who arrived home on Monday morning, haggard and exhausted. She was the only one who came back Sunday nights. I can still see her standing by our large gate with her big smile when we returned from the beach, hiding the bag of candies she had bought us, the ones Mother forbade us to eat, behind her back.

Over the years Saturnina became a reassuring presence in our family. She was there when we came back from our trips and schooling abroad. She asked questions and looked at our new clothes and gadgets. If she was ever jealous, she never showed it. Saturnina asked to keep the boxes, the wrappings, and the ribbons that came with our purchases. Her only fears for us were that Mother Earth would make our airplane fall down and that we would not return for other, unimaginable reasons.

On one of my trips home from college, she confessed that she was in love with Ismael, Mother's driver, and that he loved her too, "just like they love in the *radio-novelas*." We plotted how to break the news to Mother. Saturnina, who was then almost thirty, was afraid that Mother would not approve of the relationship because Ismael was older and whiter than she.

They married before I went back to school. Saturnina made her own wedding dress of satin and lace, like a "real bride." For her wedding day, she cut her hair and gave herself a perm. We gave her a sewing machine and a refrigerator as wedding gifts. Because she was so special, she was allowed to stay as day help. When she got pregnant, she proudly told Mother that her husband made enough money for her to stay home and be a "real mother" like her *patrona*. Eventually she and her husband saved enough money to open a small grocery store, where she still works.

Not long ago I visited Saturnina's house. It was clean and filled with the things that Mother had no longer needed. Our photographs sat next to those of her children in the place of honor on top of the TV. I saw her at Mother's funeral. She came dressed in black, still one of us.

Saturnina has not changed, but the times have. She dreams of having enough money to enable her children to learn a trade. Yet her store has iron bars to protect it from thieves and terrorists. I asked Saturnina what has happened. Reluctantly, she gave me the following answer: "It's modern times." Then she covered her face with her hands as she did years ago when she faced a difficult task. I knew to ask no more.

3

FATHER

MY FONDEST RECOLLECTION of Father is the sight of him before lunch sitting under a huge pine tree in our garden and reading the paper. The maid would bring him a whiskey, the only one of the day, which he would drink with great care. My father was very handsome. Much taller than everyone else in town, he had striking blue eyes and a wide forehead that bespoke his great intelligence. He wore suits that were made for him in Lima, of materials that came from England. He wore wide-brimmed Borsalino hats and flamboyant ties that Mother chose. He seemed larger than life to me seated in his wicker chair, a silver tray at his side, his tall glass flanked by a tiny bouquet of flowers. I watched him from the living room window and waited for him to finish the paper, when we would be allowed to join him. This time of day was our private time with Father, the most special of moments.

When we were young, he mostly quizzed us about our schoolwork. As we got older, Father began to tell us his own stories, including the one about the day his parents took him to the boat in Genoa to send him off to Peru. He explained how anxious he had been for adventure and how sad he had been to see his mother cry. I had seen pictures of him taken on that day: a thin young man, his pale face dominated by inquisitive eyes. All of nineteen years old, he was dressed in a suit that still had room for him to grow.

"I left because I was badly behaved at school," he explained. "My poor mother did not know what to do with me. I kept getting into trouble — not big trouble, just a lot of small things that made her life miserable. My father was away a lot on business, and my mother understood all along that I needed a different life. We lived in a small town where there was not very much of a future for young people. I always read adventure books, about Marco Polo and Magellan, and I wanted to discover my own continents. It was my mother's idea that I come to Peru. She had a relative who had come here, and she wrote to him. My father would not hear of it, but my mother told him that if Queen Isabella could sell her jewels to pay for Columbus's voyage, she could sell her jewelry for me. I loved my mother so much for being brave and sending me away, knowing that perhaps she would not see me again. My anguish was such that when I got to the boat, I could barely leave the cabin. I felt I had deserted her.

"Soon I began to make friends with the sailors. They taught me to play cards and told me about their adventures. It was a long trip. By the time I got to Peru, I knew a lot about the grown-up world.

"I had no idea what I was going to find when I got here. When I saw this brown, flat coast, I thought I would suffocate. My country was so green and fertile, the hills lush, as if they were made of velvet. Peru was so raw and large, so untouched by the hand of man. Where everything in Italy was cultivated and inhabited, everything in Peru was empty. The Andes were bigger and taller than the Alps, the Pacific rougher than the Mediterranean, the smells stronger, the insects bigger. I bought myself a horse and rode out to places where no one had been before, something previously inconceivable to me.

"Years later, I went back to Italy on vacation and found your mother. I wanted a wife who knew the way I had lived growing up. As I got older, I missed the things of my childhood, the simple things, like the way my mother's food tasted, or the way the beds were made in Italy, or the way the flowers were arranged. When I asked your mother to come to Peru with me, I tried to prepare her for all the strangeness of this land. It was hard for her. She missed the pine trees, the rhododendrons, the sky dotted with the white clouds of Italy. By the time we got ready to build this house, your mother, like me, loved both countries, and with this garden she created a special mélange of the two.

"Your mother taught me to appreciate a different kind of beauty here. She saw the pink and grays, the lavender and the copper tints that colored the landscape. She noticed the thin air, sprinkled with clean, almost imperceptible grains of sand and rich with the odor of dry earth and roots. She taught me to discover the secret life of the desert, the hundreds of creatures that awaken in the cool of the night to break the unearthly silence. She even found beauty in the muddy stream behind our house, once she learned the miraculous Incan method of apportioning water to make so many things grow.

"We found good people here, kind people who let us share the wealth of their country, who invited us to their homes and taught us their ways while respecting ours. People like Señorita Luisa's father, whose family had lived here for generations and who could trace his blood to Indian *caciques* and Spanish *conquistadores*. Humble people, like the Indians in the marketplaces, their sad faces marked by years of suffering, still trusting, still willing to work for us. We also found other foreigners — the English, the Germans, and the Japanese, all brave people who built railroads through the Andes, started airlines, and put up oil refineries. We saw some fail, like the young Italian bride who came to marry someone she did not know and was so unhappy that she went back with the money we collected for her.

"We lucky ones arrived in Peru with a need for adventure. Others came simply to make a living. Most of us did not think much about what we would find. The country seduced us, and we made our lives here. We tried to accommodate business ideas from the old country to Peru. My friend Carlo Rossi grew olives that needed little water and sent them to Europe to make oil, and Don Enrico Capra, the son of Italian artisans, thought of ways to work with Peruvian silver instead of brass. Instead of exporting bars of silver, he exported beautiful objects.

"As a child, I liked to trade things — my mother's biscuits for foreign stamps, and later foreign stamps for travel and adventure books. So when I came here, I continued to do what I had always done. I saw that cotton was plentiful and of good quality in Peru, and I found places in Europe where it was needed. In Peru we needed trucks and cars, so I brought them here to sell. This became my business, moving things from one place to the other."

Sitting under the pine tree, Father seemed so different from the businessman we saw in his office. There he sat behind a huge desk covered with neat piles of papers. He was always accompanied by someone who was taking dictation or discussing business. Or we saw him in command as he took us through his warehouses filled with hides, bails of cotton, and barrels of olives waiting to be loaded into trucks, everything in a perilous state of movement. At home, under the pine tree, everything was peaceful.

Often he would receive people in this garden setting. These visits annoyed Mother. "What do they want from him this time?" she would ask in an irritated voice. Toward the end of his life, when I returned home for my college vacations, I noticed that more and more people came to talk to him, having conversations in which we did not participate. We knew them to be serious private matters. A gentle, reserved man, he was a great listener, in whose presence everyone felt protected. He became an arbiter in our town, a trusted sage who was able to understand the local mores and add his Old World wisdom. When he walked through the streets, he was greeted as *padrino*. He had many godchildren, to whom he was generous. On his birthday, they arrived at the house with an eclectic assortment of presents: blue canaries in delicate cages, special cakes made of coconut and honey, or Parker 51 pens, all the rage at the time. After he died, we learned the magnitude of his generosity. People stopped me on the street to tell me how he had paid their medical bills, put their sons through trade school, or acted as a loving matchmaker.

4

A STORY ABOUT FATHER

THIS STORY was told to me by a stranger shortly after Father died. I was walking by myself in the large *alameda*. It was noon, and the streets were almost empty. Feeling as though I were being followed, I turned, to see a man a few steps behind me. Sensing my apprehension, he rushed to explain: "Excuse me, señorita, for my indiscretion, but I wanted to express my profound sympathy for your father's death. Your father was a real *caballero*. He shall be missed in this town." I was used to being stopped on the street by people who were anxious to give me their condolences, so I thanked him and walked on.

"Let me introduce myself," he said as he extended his hand to give me a handshake. "My name is Manuel Soto. There is no reason why you should know me, but I have something very important to tell you, and you must allow me to do it." A short man in his thirties, he was what we call in Peru a *cholo*, someone of mixed blood — in his case, mostly Indian, with little European blood. He was dressed in a dark suit. A gold chain around his neck shone in the bright light. For a moment I thought he was about to ask me for money, so I kept on walking.

"I don't want anything from you," he said, and he tried to hand me a little red box.

"Please," I said, "I can't accept something from you. I don't know you."

"I know this is odd," he said nervously, "but if you give me a few minutes of your time, I might change your mind."

I could tell by his manner that he was a kind man, that he had a mission, and that nothing would stop him. "Please, go ahead," I said. "Be brief. I am expected for lunch in a few minutes."

"What I am going to tell you is about something extraordinary your father did for me and for my mother," he said. He pointed to one of the little benches in the *alameda*. We sat there together and he told me the following story.

"My mother, Rosa, was an Indian woman. She was a domestic who cooked and kept house for the same family from the age of fourteen. It was a small family, just the *patrona*, Dona Alba, and her son, Don Antenor. They lived in that old house in the *alameda* that was torn down to build the new school. You must remember it — a fine old house, with beautiful wrought iron gates covered with honeysuckle. I can still smell its sweet aroma.

"The *patrona* was a saintly woman, very religious. She was very old. My mother took complete care of her. I was born because the *patrón* and my mother committed a sin. The *patrona* arranged for me to be baptized and accepted that my mother would keep me with her. She never asked my mother who the father was. The *patrón* did not give me his name — I was an *ilegítimo*, with my mother's last name, Peres. I don't remember the old *patrona*. She died when I was three years old.

"The *patrón*, Don Antenor, kept my mother. She was his woman. Because she was a domestic, she did not move into his bedroom. At night he came to the quarters behind the kitchen that my mother and I shared. He treated her well and paid for me to go to the priests' school, which was unusual — most *ilegítimos* like me went to the public school. At school no one asked who my father was, yet everyone knew. It was hard for me. I was never invited to play in my classmates' homes, and my mother never came to school events or walked me to school, as other mothers did.

"For a while my mother and I ate our meals separately from the *patrón*. She would serve Don Antenor in the dining room and we would eat in the kitchen. He was much older than my mother and began to suffer the ills of old age. He spent more and more time in the house. I remember the *patrón* and my mother sitting in the sunroom — he read the paper while she sat quietly next to him. He grew a long white beard, which made him look older and mean. But he was kind to me. My mother did not know how to read or write, so he helped me with my schoolwork, and when we were finished he let me play the gramophone.

"At about this time, my mother moved into his bedroom and I was given the room that used to belong to his mother. We began to eat together in the dining room. It seemed so extraordinary to eat at a cloth-covered table set with silver and crystal. Mother even hired a young woman to help her with the chores. She began to call him Antenor, instead of Don Antenor. I was too young to understand what it all meant. I just started to call him Father, as I was told.

"One night the doctor had to be called. Don Antenor asked my mother to leave while the doctor visited him, but my mother stayed behind the draperies. She overheard the doctor tell him that he had only six months to live. My mother was one of those women who had learned from life to face reality head-on. She was a strong woman. She was beautiful."

At that, he produced a photograph. I saw a handsome Indian woman seated very stiffly, wearing a lace blouse, a stern look, and a forced smile. There was in her look the kind of determination and pride that I have often seen in Indian women who have made it to the middle class. It is as if they are saying, "We know who we are."

"Your mother seems very determined and intelligent," I said.

"Yes. She even learned how to read and write, when

she was fifty. She lives with God now," he responded, and quickly added, "Let me go on with my story.

"In the days after the doctor's visit there was a lot of tension. I could hear both of them talking late into the night. During the day my mother was very silent. She had seen your father visit Don Antenor, so the following Sunday, on the way to church, she went to your house. She told your father her troubles. She did not care about herself, but she knew that if Señor Antenor didn't marry her, I would always be an *ilegítimo* and would not inherit any of his money. His relatives would come and send us out of the house. My mother told me that she cried while she was saying all these things. Your father remained silent until she was finished. Then he said, 'Rosa, don't worry.'

"She also told me that your garden was beautiful, filled with flowers she had never seen, and that she had been received not like a domestic but like a lady. Your father had offered her a seat, and the maid had brought her a glass of juice.

"That same afternoon your father went to see Don Antenor. He was there for a long time. He went back several times. The following Sunday, Don Antenor called my mother and me to his room. He was dressed in his business suit, and he said solemnly, 'My friend is going to arrive in a few minutes. He is bringing the *alcalde* who is going to marry Rosa and me.' Before anyone said anything, he told us to go put on our best clothes. I did not have any fancy clothes, so I put on my school uniform. My mother was crying so much nothing could stop her. She just kept saying, 'Thank you, Virgin Mary.'

"When we got back to the living room, the *alcalde* and your father were there, and two other people I did not know, who were going to be the witnesses. The *alcalde* was very stiff, as if he were doing something he did not want to do. He opened a big book, and everyone signed several times. When all the signing was done, your father asked for the champagne, and Don Antenor opened a bottle, and the champagne spilled all over. He told my mother not to clean it, saying that she was no longer the maid, that she was Señora Soto and I was Manuel Soto. My mother was so grateful and happy all she could do was cry and say thank you to everyone. After they all left, Don Antenor opened his safe and pulled out a ring with a red stone. My mother wore it all her life. She said she had seen her old *patrona* wear it. He gave me two gold coins from Chile. He said he had bought them from a Chilean family when they had to go back to Chile in 1929, after the plebiscite.

"When I told my teacher at school that I had a new name, she said, 'I know. Your mother gave Don Antenor a potion so that he would marry her.' I said nothing about this to anyone. I knew that not much had changed for me.

"Don Antenor died not too long after that. I remember the funeral. There were only four of us. Your father and the priest came. Your father told me to take care of my mother. My father left us plenty of money. When the time came for me to go to the university, we sold the house and moved to Lima. We lived lonely lives there, too, until I met Juana, my wife. She came from a good old-fashioned large family, and they welcomed us. She doesn't want to tell our children that I am an *ilegítimo*. I will tell them when they are older. I am more modern, and I don't think these things matter anymore."

Soto became very nervous, and with a shaky voice he added, "When I heard that your father had died, I wanted to come to Tacna and tell your family this story." I detected a strain in his voice, as if he were saying something he was not sure he should. He anxiously added, "I followed your father's advice. I took care of my mother, and now I take care of my family. I am so thankful to him for making my mother an honest woman, something my own father did only because of him."

There was a long pause. Then he pulled the little box out of his pocket and handed it to me. "Now, take it, please," he begged. "They were in Don Antenor's safe. My mother thought they were too fancy for her to wear. My wife feels the same. We want you to have them."

Inside the box was a pair of delicate gold filigree

earrings, which I still wear for special occasions. These earrings have become a tribute to my father, and to this episode, which is so revealing of the kind of man he was. I never tire of telling this story to my children, and they never tire of hearing it.

5

MY PERUVIAN SCHOOL

I REMEMBER VIVIDLY my first day of school. I was seven years old. I awakened earlier than usual and dressed in my school uniform, a pleated blue wool skirt and white cotton shirt. My mother made a special breakfast that day. Instead of toast, she let me have stone cake, a hard, not-too-sweet cake, which made great company for her jams. It was Mother's way of trying to make the day special. It was special, all right; I had no idea of what awaited me at school.

Unlike my home life, which was filled with magical qualities that gave my childhood so much happiness, my school life was filled with incidents that seemed like torture. When it came to which school I would attend, my parents felt they had no choice but to send me to the one private school in town for girls. The public schools were so bad that even families of modest means made every effort to send their children to the private school. Thus the student body was a cross-section of my town's population, much like the students in the public school's.

The school property was surrounded by a tall wall which I had passed many times. I expected the building inside to be something very special, and I was disappointed to find instead an old rundown house. Only the statues of saints that had been placed in front of the classrooms made it look like a normal school. It was staffed by seven Italian nuns, with the help of some Peruvian teachers. Since the nuns regarded sports as unladylike, there were not even any playing fields. The only available spaces other than the classrooms were a large courtyard, for our patriotic displays, and a chapel, for the religious ones.

Both my parents drove me to school that first morning. Unhappily for me, the school bus arrived just as we got out of Father's brand-new car, a large green Mercury that I had loved until that fateful day. When I felt the eyes of the entire student body looking not at me but at our car, I understood for the first time in my life the kind of envy that was to make my school life very hard.

The mother superior came to greet us. I was relieved that she was so welcoming. She led us into her office, a small room dominated by a large desk and a crucifix on the wall. She asked my parents to sit. To me she said, "Students are never allowed to sit in my office. This is the way I teach them respect for authority." She ignored me as she delivered a long monologue about the virtues of her school and the need "to involve the generosity of those few parents who could afford to be generous." I felt so bereft. I was the one going to her school, and her interest was only in my parents. My heart felt small, and a great lump parked itself in my throat. I made an enormous effort not to cry, because I felt she wanted me to.

When my parents left, she asked me to wait for her and went off. I could hear the whole school in the courtyard, saying the morning prayers and singing the national anthem. I thought she had forgotten me, but she simply had a different plan. She came to fetch me, saying that since I was "such a special student," she would take me to my classroom and introduce me to my classmates herself.

As we crossed the large courtyard, the faces of my fellow students crowded at their classroom windows to stare at us. My classroom was at the far end, and with everyone staring, the crossing felt interminable. The nun who was to be my teacher stood at the door. I curtsied to her, the way I had been taught to do. The mother superior said loudly, so that everyone could hear, "We don't do that here. You have come here to learn to be like everyone else."

My teacher was a young nun and immediately understood my predicament. With a certain defiance, for which she might have been reprimanded later, she told the mother superior, "Thank you for bringing over my new student," and grabbing me by the hand, she took me into the room. There, sitting behind small wooden desks, were my thirty classmates. Their dark eyes were upon me. They appeared to be a hostile army ready for attack. Because of Mother's tutoring, I had been skipped to the second grade, and my classmates were two years older than me. I was told to sit next to a girl named Rosa.

When we were sent out for recess, I told my teacher that I would rather stay in the classroom. She called Rosa and asked her to take me with her. We sat in a corner of the courtyard by ourselves. Rosa and I became fast friends, a friendship that has lasted until today. She was the daughter of the head of the army garrison, the most important government figure in my town; that made her different, like me. Her family had moved to Tacna a year before, and for a whole school year she had endured childish hostilities. In sharing our miseries, we discovered the territory of friendship.

Rosa, too, lived in a large house with servants. She, too, was driven to school in a fancy car. Her parents, too, were the subjects of the mother superior's attentions. Rosa had been brought up very much the way I had. Very soon we were going to each other's home to do homework together, and we persuaded our parents to let us walk to school. Until her father was transferred to another town, we were inseparable. Together we learned to protect each other. We even stood up to Elena, the toughest girl in the class.

Elena was the illegitimate daughter of a *contrabandista*, a smuggler. A loud, large girl, she was the only one who had the nerve to call us "princesses" to our faces. Elena also discovered my secret love for an Indian boy named Manuel. Rosa and I knew that Elena had a crush on Manuel herself. We got Saturnina to get us a special root that made women unattractive to men. We left it under her books and watched as she discovered it. Because the entire class had a crush on Manuel, she never found out who did it.

Elena was very smart. We competed for the top grades in the class, and when I did better than she, her reaction was, "How much did your father pay for you to be ahead of me?" She was also the favorite of the mother superior, who held her up to the class as an exemplary student. Rosa later told me that Elena's mother saved enough money to send her to law school in Lima. There she met and married a Leninist professor, and they went to Cuba to be trained as terrorists. Recently Rosa sent me a clipping that said that Elena had been captured as one of a terrorist group that had blown up a private school and hurt many children. I wonder what the mother superior would think of her pet student now.

I wanted so badly to be accepted at school, to be like everyone else, but that never happened. I longed for the school bell to ring and for it to be time to go home. I longed for Sundays, when we went to our beach house and saw no one outside the family. There were moments when I wished I could just stay home. Often I pretended to be sick, but Mother was too smart for that. There were brief interludes when things seemed to march along fairly smoothly, and then something like my parents' Italian Day party would come along and my peace would end. I had to endure the hurtful insults of the girls whose parents had not been invited, who targeted me with their families' anger. I was called "daughter of Italian thieves" and other such insults. I knew that many of my classmates reveled in the mother superior's injustice toward me. Although at home my parents more than made up for this mistreatment, it contributed to their eventual decision to send me away to school, knowing full well that I might not return to Peru.

Last year I attended a mass said for Mother in the school's chapel. Very little had changed. The nuns looked younger, the building looked older, and in the restless young faces of the students I spotted many more Elenas than Rosas.

6

FALLING IN LOVE

THE SUMMER before I was sent to school in England was the summer I first fell in love. I was fourteen years old. The object of my affection, of course, was Manuel, the heartthrob of the class. He was the dark-haired and green-eyed embodiment of Señorita Luisa's brothers; at least that's what I imagined. My friends thought he was very macho. He wore tight pants and a *habanera*, a loose shirt that the men in my country wear to hide their bellies, though Manuel wore his to show off his virility. He wore it unbuttoned, with a gold medal shining on his dark chest. He walked the way men do when they know women look at them, and as he walked, he whistled the most recent romantic tunes. He knew how many young women were in love with him and treated all of us with equal superiority. Every day I waited to catch a glimpse of him as he passed my house on his way to his after-school work. I spent hours in front of the mirror preparing for the possibility of a furtive encounter. I longed for him to look my way, and I fantasized that he took me to the movies and held my hand in the dark.

Manuel came from a very modest family, so modest that they could not afford to send him to high school.

The fact that he had a part-time job did not seem to perturb him. He worked at the local hardware store, and spent his few moments of free time walking up and down the *alameda*, showing himself off. I kept my feelings secret for fear my parents would find out.

A few times I got up my courage and found an excuse to go inside the store where Manuel worked. There was nothing for me to buy there, so I pretended to be looking for the gardener or bought a useless light bulb with my meager allowance. Manuel pretended not to notice me. Elena, who was reputed to be Manuel's real girlfriend, accused me of going to the hardware store to steal her sweetheart. She told me that gringas like me should stick to gringos and not fall in love with *cholos*. Her threats to tell my mother forced me to live in fear that my parents would discover my infatuation. I could not sleep or eat, and my youthful longings became confused with my fear of being caught.

I confessed my unhappiness to Saturnina. Unwillingly, she agreed to help me. She told me to wrap a canary feather in lovage, tie a pink ribbon around it, and hide it in his path. He would surely pay attention to me then. Saturnina also agreed to deliver a note to him. It took me three nights to compose my missive, but it was never delivered. My mother must have extracted a confession from Saturnina, because one day when I came back from school, I was greeted by an icy hello from my mother. She showed me the note, and before I had time to utter a word, she asked me to join her in the kitchen.

The house seemed unusually quiet that day, and as I followed her, I noticed that all of the household help was gone. A dead hen, feathers and all, had been placed in the middle of a kitchen counter. I looked at my mother in bewilderment. In the cool voice she sometimes used, she announced, "If you are so much in love with Manuel, I think you should learn how women of his class live. Please pluck the hen, clean it, and cut it. I have left written instructions." She pointed to a piece of paper next to the hen and left the room. In my misery I hoped that Saturnina would appear, but she had been given the day off, too.

The hen and I looked at each other for a long time. When I realized that I had no choice, I plunged into my messy task. It took hours to accomplish. The hen had an endless number of stubbornly attached feathers. A few times she landed on the floor. The confrontation with the entrails was a more complicated matter. I was sick to my stomach twice before I got through. When I was done, I went to my room in a state of furious capitulation. All my tender feelings for Manuel had turned to rage against my mother. She had won.

The next morning, no one said anything about the incident. The cook gave me a compassionate look, and the maids giggled when they saw me. Saturnina told me she could not give me advice any longer. She had come very close to losing her job.

A few years ago I ran into Manuel, who then worked at the post office. As he sold me some stamps, it was hard for me to conceive that he had been the subject of my adoration. He had lost all his bravado, his habanera hid a large belly, and two gold teeth had replaced the gold medal.

7

MOTHER

MY FONDEST MEMORY of Mother is of her waiting for us to return from school. She almost always waited at the top of the steps that led to the house. As I came through the gate and saw her in the distance, she appeared magnificent to me. Tall and slender, she dressed in pastel silk dresses, her long brown hair resting gently on her shoulders. She waved as she waited, and then held her arms open to give me a hug. Mother had the softest pale skin, and her blue eyes were resplendent below her long, gently curved eyebrows. She wore no makeup, nor ornaments, except for a pair of large pearl earrings. She smelled of fresh flowers, and her hugs made me feel safe, as if I had arrived at a sheltered harbor after the storms at school.

After our hellos, we followed her to the study, where

we ate our midafternoon snack of small sandwiches and warm milk and discussed our homework. After intricate negotiations, we would settle on exactly how long it should take us to complete each task, and that was the amount of time we were allowed. She thought that this would teach us to plan our time and organize our priorities. To this day, I never approach a task without planning it in my mind beforehand.

Mother stayed in the library with us while we did our schoolwork. She sat by the window in a large chair covered in soft blue velvet and knitted while she gazed out over her garden. She knitted very fast. I can still hear the sound of her needles, like the steady drums of a guardian army. When the homework was done, Mother reviewed it. When we needed help, we were always told to look up the information in the encyclopedia or the spelling in the dictionary. She never provided the answer herself.

Until the children in my family reached their thirteenth birthday, they ate dinner before Father came home from work. Mother kept us company, and it was then that we discussed our school days. She had no tolerance for our complaints, which were plentiful. It was only shortly before she died that she admitted to me that she knew how miserable I was in school. There was no other choice in my town; my misery was the burden of being a member of one of the very few affluent families. When I was young, I envied friends whose mothers seemed willing to listen to the "injustices" they suffered at school. Now I understand that Mother had no choice but to compensate by creating an enchanting home and by making our lives there very special.

To the outside world, Mother was a mystery, an impression she liked to cultivate with her silence. I heard stories about Mother from my classmates at school and from the maids. Because she was much younger than Father and because he had been for so long the most eligible bachelor in town, the stories were abundant. My favorite one was that she had been brought up by gypsies and Father had fallen under her spell when he saw her. He had bought her from the gypsy king for so much gold that everyone in the tribe was able to get gold teeth.

Someone once told me a version I dreaded: that Father had stolen her from an old man to whom she was married. That story made me into an illegitimate child, like so many children in my town. As I grew older, I liked to believe the story my friend Ana told me, that Mother had been an orphan brought up by nuns in a convent. This, it turned out, was not far from the truth.

On my fifteenth birthday, Mother gave me a special gift. The afternoon was warm, and the sun was just beginning to set. The copious pink flowers of the oleanders shimmered gently in the breeze, scenting the tender air with a honey aroma. Mother and I sat under Father's pine tree. She asked me to sit close to her, and in her soft, vibrant voice, she gave me the gift of her story. "You are old enough now," she said, "to know my history. There is nothing secret about it. Your father and I felt we should wait until you could understand it, though, because until the part when I meet your father, it is sometimes very sad.

"My own father was much older than my mother. I never knew him, because he died shortly after I was born. He was a very successful businessman and left my mother a fortune. He had worked hard to make his money, and he never gave himself the time to enjoy it. We lived in a big villa on the Italian Riviera, a tall house that stood in the middle of a large formal garden.

"My mother was a beautiful woman. She let her beauty guide her life, and it brought her only sadness. My memories of my mother are like snapshots. She came and went from the house at odd hours. Sometimes she was gone for long periods of time. Often she disappeared without even saying goodbye, leaving behind a trail of her strong perfume, or tiny pieces of the feather boas she wore.

"I had a series of nannies. No one liked to work for my mother. Spoiled and pampered by her many admirers because of her beauty, she treated the people who worked for her badly. I don't remember very much about those early years. When I was five years old, my mother took me to a convent and left me there. She had a distant relative who was a nun, and I lived with her order until I married your father.

"The nuns were good to me. The convent was really the only home I ever knew. My mother did not visit me often, though when she did, she brought me expensive presents from her trips. Her visits were short. She couldn't stand to be around the nuns, she said. They made her nervous. But I was lucky, because they were good for small children. The nuns with whom I lived were part of a nursing order that worked in a hospital next to the convent. A nun from another convent came to tutor me each day.

"I was happy at the convent. The nuns were my only friends. I went to Mass with them every morning and prayed the vespers. From the nuns I learned to love and to fear God. The mother superior taught me that religion comes from the heart, not from institutions. She said that it was more important to be true to God than to pray rosaries or attend Mass. I learned to play the piano, to work in the nuns' elaborate garden, to cook, and to speak Latin.

"The mother superior was my special friend. She was a tall woman with a large forehead and red cheeks, and she laughed often. I learned a lot from Mother Superior, and I came to think of her as a mother. I can still remember the day I arrived at the convent. She was very kind to me. At night, she made sure I brushed my teeth and said my prayers, and then she tucked me into bed.

"She was the only nun who went out — to shop and to visit the people who supported the convent. She often took me with her. She bought my clothes, and when I got older she took me to the hairdresser to have my hair cut. She also took care of what she called my 'reading life.' By that she meant that I had to learn about life beyond the convent from books. She told me that some of the books she gave me were only for me, not to be read by the other nuns, who were better off not knowing some things about the outside world.

"It's somewhat sad to think of a young child learning about the world from books. Still, I am grateful that she offered me this window beyond the predictable and sheltered life of the convent. When I finally left it to marry your father, I found that I had a passion for the real world, and I have never had enough of it.

"Mother Superior understood that it was not my vocation to become a nun. When I was eighteen years old, she enrolled me in a course to become a nurse. It was rare in those days for young women like me to have a profession, but my mother had spent the money Father had left us, and I had to learn to support myself. The mother superior found the best school for me. I had to go by train every day.

"Early in my schooling I met your father on the train. I saw him a number of times before he talked to me. He was so handsome, so elegant. I knew little about the world, and when he finally spoke to me, I felt that my face was on fire. We met on the train for many trips. He made me feel comfortable and happy. He told me about Peru and his life there, which from his descriptions sounded wonderful and adventurous. He brought me chocolates and cologne. The train ride took an hour each way, so we got to know each other well. He never told me what he did while I was in classes. Afterward, he was always there at the entrance to the station, pretending to read the paper.

"One day, a few weeks after our first encounter, he was not on the train. I was in a state of despair, and arrived back at the convent in tears. Waiting for me at the entrance was the mother superior, who ran to me and hugged me very hard. 'I am happy for you,' she said. 'My prayers have been answered. You will be a good wife and mother.'

"Your father was in the parlor. The mother superior disappeared. It was then that your father asked me to marry him. I learned later that he had asked for my hand a week before, and that the mother superior had questioned her contacts about him, to make sure he was a good and honorable man. That evening your father and I drank a bottle of champagne with the mother superior. She was so happy. She said again and again, 'The best husband is the kind the Lord finds. The Lord found yours.'

"It was 1939, and the war loomed in our lives. We had to get married quickly or the war would make it impossible for us to go to Peru for a long time. The mother superior went with me to meet your father's family. It must have seemed odd to them to have me arrive with a nun as my only family. They were kind, warm people who received me openly. Your father's mother was especially kind. She treated me as if she had known me all her life. She came along with the mother superior to help me buy my wedding gown, which was made of satin and lace. The mother superior paid for my trousseau. I don't know where the money came from, but she bought me the most beautiful things we could find.

"We were married in the convent's chapel. My mother did not come to the wedding. It was an early spring evening. The air was filled with good signs — birds singing, flowers blooming, a gentle rain falling. It was a beautiful wedding. The nuns had filled the chapel with white roses. They made the wedding cake and sang for us. I had no family there, but your father's large family filled the chapel. Before the ceremony, your father's mother took me aside and gave me her engagement ring, this lovely ruby ring I have never taken off. She called me Daughter and asked me to think of her as a new mother. I loved her so for being so welcoming. I never saw her again, for she died a few months later. When we left for our honeymoon, the mother superior gave me her Bible, the one I read to you. I was sad to leave the convent, but I was filled with the happiness your father gave me.

"At the harbor, my mother was waiting for us. She was dressed all in black, as if she were going to a funeral. A gentleman was with her, but we were not introduced. All she said to me was, 'Be happy.' She had brought a bouquet of flowers for me and one flower for your father's lapel. It was her way of saying that she wished us happiness. I saw her crying as the boat pulled away.

"Your father and I sailed the long ocean. He tried to prepare me for our life in Peru. At first it was only my love for him that made this place bearable. It seemed so arid, so raw. I could not speak the language, the food seemed to burn my mouth, and the air was filled with dust. But I believed what your father told me, that at first it had seemed strange to him, too, and that he had learned to like it and then to love it. He was right. We built our lives together, and soon you were born, and then the world made only happy sounds.

"The mother superior died shortly after I came to Peru. The convent where I grew up was destroyed during the war. My mother is old now. Her beauty is gone, and she is left with very little. She writes to me and tells me to live a different life from hers. Her letters are long and sad. Sometimes I can't read them. She is very lonely. Your father and I have asked her to come here, but she refuses. I don't blame her for any-thing, and neither should you. No one should be blamed for how they choose to live."

8
MOTHER'S COOKING

OUR KITCHEN was a large room covered with white and blue tiles. It had generous windows that opened onto the garden, ample counters, and a large table in the middle, where the maids congregated for their meals and, during their free hours, listened to the *radio-novelas.* The kitchen was a laboratory in constant operation, where everyone worked to produce Mother's experiments. Mother's cooking was a reflection of her approach to life, filled with enthusiasm and desire for the new. I often think that it must have been born of the monotony of her early life in the convent.

Even simple breakfasts of hot chocolate and toast were the products of elaborate preparation. The jams were made at home from fruit so ripe no sugar was used. There were many varieties: mulberry, apricot, tangerine, and Mother's specialty, tomato jam, made with bitter almonds with an unusual, piquant flavor.

Mother's cuisine combined the cooking of her native Italy, learned from the nuns, the cooking of Peru, and French recipes from her magazines. It was a fragrant and delicate cuisine, in which no flavor or ingredient dominated but they all blended in pleasing, unexpected harmony.

Food arrived at the table as a small triumph that Mother loved to share with her family, especially with Father, who was an abstemious but sophisticated eater. To the corn dishes she learned to prepare in Peru, she added her own touches, such as a bit of saffron and some pine nuts. Her pastas, which as a child I loved to see roll out of the cutter, were a specialty all her own. Sometimes they were filled with porcini mushrooms from Italy, fava beans mashed with sweet potatoes and onions, or eggplant and fresh oregano. At other times they were served with one of an endless variety of sauces, made with zucchini flowers, sea urchins, veal marrow, baby avocados, or walnuts — some heavy and wintery, some light and spirited, depending on the season and the ripeness of the vegetables. Even the simple tomato-and-basil sauce was special. It was only made on those few days of summer when the tomatoes were perfectly ripe.

In the summer we ate grilled fish and octopus with tender salads and stuffed vegetables. When it got cool, a rarity in the desert, Mother, nostalgic for Italy, would serve pork roasts surrounded by potatoes in a spicy pepper sauce. For Easter we had baked stuffed baby goat, succulent with the scent of rosemary, accompanied by artichokes and peas. The Christmas turkey arrived at the table stuffed with chestnuts, wild rice, and sage, surrounded by asparagus. Desserts were the culmination of every meal. I can still see the mountains of tiny puff pastries stuffed with a cherimoya cream and held together by caramel, the Napoleon cake layered with guava sauce, crunchy and light, and the home-made ice creams rich with chunks of pomegranates and peaches.

The ingredients that arrived at Mother's kitchen were the result of an elaborate gathering process. A great majority came from our own garden; the rest Mother found in the marketplace, where she became an expert on foods both local and imported. There, like the rest of the women of my town, she became a huntress in pursuit of perfection. Mother knew how to tell the ripeness of a pineapple by the texture of its skin, the freshness of a fish by the amount of moisture in its eyes, and the hotness of a pepper by the shade of its skin.

Twice a week, early in the morning, she went to the market. I loved going with her and watching her move among the piles of fresh fruits and vegetables. Fruits included papayas and guavas from the jungle, apples and peaches from Chile, sweet juicy grapes, oranges, and pomegranates from the local farms — products of the desert that never knew morning dew and were ripened only by the caress of the sun. The vegetable counters were equally plentiful. Mother learned to distinguish among the thirty-odd varieties of potatoes available. Purple ones were to be used with cheese sauces, porous yellow ones for stews, firm white ones for frying. She pinched, sniffed, and weighed the vegetables until she found the right ones. As a child I tried hard to learn these skills, but when my turn came to use them as a young bride in America, they were useless to me. I discovered that tomatoes came in plastic boxes, apples were sealed in plastic bags, and corn was only sold frozen.

Mother was at her best on Fridays, when the fishermen's wives took over the market. They brought with them the bounties of the Pacific: tiny fish such as anchovies and sardines, huge slabs of swordfish and bonito, and the fruits of the sea, urchins, clams, crabs, and lobsters. Because we had a refrigerator at home and could store a large amount of fish, Mother was a favored customer. The fishwives saved her corbina to make ceviche, the Peruvian kind, with lime juice and olive oil, and clams of all sizes and colors for her risottos.

Mother was good at bargaining. She would struggle to find something wrong with a vegetable in order to get a good price, or she would tactfully point out that someone else was selling the same merchandise for less. All the women of my town bargained. It was a chance for the housewives to display a skill, to feel the power of their knowledge.

The market was also where housewives exchanged gossip and recipes. I still smile to myself when I remember the day Mother overheard two housewives talking about an unusual way to prepare a turkey for a gourmet death. She rushed home to persuade Father and Pablo, our gardener, to try out the new method. For a week the two men force-fed a turkey five spoonfuls of brandy a day followed by a handful of nuts. Every time I eat turkey, I remember Mother's bird wobbling happily in a drunken stupor. When we finally ate it, it had a wonderful flavor that I have never encountered since.

When the marketing was done, two hours after Mother began, she filled the car with baskets and we headed for home. As soon as we got there, it was time to start the interminable process of scrubbing and drying the food. Later everything would be wrapped in white paper, labeled, and stored.

Mother was like a dancer in the kitchen. She appeared about an hour before mealtime, after everything was already washed and chopped. Everyone was on alert, waiting for the magician who would mix and stir everything together to create a *tour de force*. She moved swiftly and intuitively, led by her internal music. Sometimes she followed a recipe carefully, concentrating intently. Then, everyone knew to be very quiet.

She never tasted anything, but seemed to make decisions based on the color and fragrance of the food. When everything was done, she would ring the old church bell on the patio to announce that the meal would be served. Radiantly, she would wait for her family, beaming with the pleasure of having put together a good meal.

Meals were served in our dining room, which overlooked the green lawn bordered with flowers. It was a room suffused in light. The tablecloths were beautifully pressed, the silver and china resplendent. At the center of the table, a large bowl of flowers, usually sweet peas or roses, gently caught the tones of the tablecloth. From the windows we could see the hummingbirds having their own feast in the hibiscus flowers, and we would hear canaries on the patio in the distance.

After lunch we took long walks in the garden, accompanied by our guardian Doberman dogs. Soon Pablo would arrive through the large colonial gate. As Mother's dedicated partner, he never questioned her agricultural experiments. When Mother returned from her trips abroad, she brought seeds and cuttings, which Pablo patiently nourished into bloom. Every time a new flower grew, it was cause for celebration. When the first nasturtium opened or the first raspberry ripened, Pablo would just shake his head and murmur, "A miracle."

He and Mother made an unusual pair. Mother moved

with the speed of light; Pablo moved slowly, as if in a perpetual state of tiredness. He was the only person I ever knew who could sleep standing up. When we were young, we loved to wake him up. Yet Pablo is still there. Now almost eighty-five years old, he has worked for my family for more than fifty years and knows the history of every plant and every tree in the garden.

When I saw him last year, it broke my heart to hear him apologize for the garden's looking so overgrown. Together we cut white roses — Mother's favorites, the most beautiful and fragrant of all roses — to take to my parents' graves.

9

MY TACNA

MY TACNA sprouted from the Atacama Desert in the south of Peru and was built by the oasis of a small river that snaked down from the Andes. The forbidding mountains reigned in the distance, snow-capped, defiant, an impenetrable barrier that stopped the abundant water of the jungle to the east from reaching our dry land. The Atacama is the driest desert in the world — not even cacti dare to grow there — and we fought a constant battle against its dust.

The town's existence depended on water from the river, a river that could be torrential in the months when it rained in the mountains and completely dry in years of drought. The water ebbed and flowed through town via a series of aqueducts designed by the Incas centuries before. Each house would get water once every two weeks, depending on the phases of the moon.

Sometimes our water would come at night and we children would be allowed to stay up to watch. A town functionary called the water master would release a series of crude wooden gates that funneled the water directly to our garden. Water was so precious that people went to extremes to protect it. On watering day, our gardener took a gun when he went to check the water master's work and made sure that no one was interfering with the path of the water to our property.

Once planted and watered, plants thrived. It was as if the ground were waiting to burst into life. Our desert soil was so fertile, my father said, that if we only had rain, we would be the richest country in the world. Later, when the town began irrigating its land with water pumped in from mountain lakes and underground wells, Tacna became famous for its succulent, flavorful vegetables.

Apart from the colors of the plants and flowers, the city was brown, from the light brown dust of the desert to the soft pink- and yellow-tinged browns of the adobe walls and the dark mud roofs. Tacna was a quiet place that moved to its own rhythms, which had changed very slowly, if at all, through the centuries. Everyone knew everyone else. The arrival of a stranger was a great event; such was the arrival of my father from Italy in 1917, and of his young bride in 1939. "When your mother arrived from the homeland," Ana's mother told me, "we all cut our hair to look like hers, we copied her dresses, and we bribed her maids to tell us what she served for dinner."

Tacna was a compact town, clean, restful, with streets covered in cobblestones and bordered by palm trees. Tiny gardens with colorful flowers bloomed sporadically. Most people lived in attached houses built near the street, with large patios and back yards crowded with chickens, little gardens, and laundry flapping in the dusty breeze. The houses were drafty, and their mud roofs were shaped like pointed brown hats that together looked like a rippled brown zig-zag against the blue sky. The larger buildings — hospitals, schools, and government offices — were also low structures, larger versions of the domestic architecture.

The center of town was the Plaza de Armas. Compared to the rest of Tacna, it was an enormous space. At one end stood the unfinished and unused cathedral, like a phantom made of stone. It appeared incredibly tall compared to most of the buildings that composed the town. Later, when it was finished, it became the pride of our city. Designed by Gustave Eiffel at a time when Tacna had been prosperous, the cathedral was a symbol of sophistication.

Eiffel had also designed the fountain that sat in the center of the plaza, which was usually dry. The most important resident of the plaza was Christopher Columbus. "I couldn't believe it," Mother used to say. "I came all the way from Genoa, expecting to find exotic heroes, and I ran into him again." Our Columbus was made of white marble. He was short and stocky, and as he gazed into the distance, looking for other new worlds, his face collected dust. Once a year, for his day, the local firemen would give him a shower and place wreaths of flowers at his feet.

At the other end of the Plaza de Armas stood our only moviehouse. Movies were advertised by bright posters of our idols in passionate embraces. My friend Ana told me that the bishop had objected to the low necklines of the stars and for that reason a large sign, FOR ADULTS ONLY, covered the women's cleavage. It was a favorite pastime of the young men to unglue these signs. One of the many sins the nuns cautioned us against at school was looking at body parts, the parts that decent people kept covered.

At six o'clock the scratchy theater gramophone would play a march announcing that the movies were about to start. Ana called it "the march to watch the sinful." How we envied those who could attend the movies. Even today, movies have an air of forbidden pleasure for me. Ana, who married the son of the moviehouse owner, jokes about having fallen in love so that she could go to the movies.

On Sunday mornings the plaza became the social center of the town. The local band played the latest tunes under a canopy of purple bougainvillea. The older people sat on the white benches while the younger ones showed off their most recent fashions. Marriages were made, affairs exposed, politics discussed. Later on, in the early afternoon, the wealthier townspeople left and the household help and the laborers populated the plaza. A looser feeling permeated the air. No band was set up, but occasionally, when he was in a good mood, the owner of the moviehouse would play Peruvian waltzes on the gramophone. Otherwise the afternoon crowd moved to its own mystifying cadences.

The Tacneños were a fiercely patriotic people who liked to recount their history. One of my father's friends, an older man named Don Demetrio, who dressed in white and sported a red carnation in his lapel, told long stories of Tacna's "most heroic moment," the War of the Pacific. He referred to Tacna as "the predilect daughter of Peru," who "had fought hard against those Chilean thieves who robbed Peru of its rich nitrate territories." Through his descriptions, this nineteenth-century war became so vivid to me that when I came to America, it seemed impossible that no one had heard of it.

The Chileans had marched all the way to Lima. Our army was smaller and poorer, and even though my countrymen fought bravely until the end, the country was devastated. Don Demetrio told us how when the war ended, the Tacneños refused to capitulate to Chilean rule. When the Chileans occupied Tacna, entire families left, abandoning their homes. Those who stayed refused to send their children to Chilean schools and sent them instead to clandestine schools operated by Peruvian loyalists.

My favorite story was about Maria Eugenia, a Peruvian beauty who carried on a secret love affair with a Chilean officer. When her family discovered her betrayal, she was sent away to Lima to live with relatives. The officer committed suicide, and Maria Eugenia returned home but never left the house again. I knew the house where she still lived during my childhood, although I never saw her. A friend of mine who claimed to have seen her told me that she had gone blind from so much crying.

"They forgot us in the capital," Don Demetrio recounted indignantly. "They forgot us until 1929, until they asked the gringos of America to come to our help!" (As seemed to happen so often, salvation came from the Americans of my dreams.) A General Lassiter was sent to conduct a referendum, and Tacna voted to go back to what Don Demetrio called "the womb of the mother country." According to him, the general was tall and handsome, so handsome that the local girls had to be kept at home so they wouldn't fall in love with him.

One of the battles of the War of the Pacific had been fought on a hill behind the cemetery at the end of town. There stood a monument, a simple pyramid inscribed with the names of those who had died in battle. As children, we visited it occasionally. Not having lived the realities of war, we found it a romantic sight. One day a new reality struck home. One of my brother's classmates found a live grenade just beneath the surface of the ground. It exploded, and he lost a leg.

We were taught rituals as ways to manifest our patriotism. At school each morning we sang the national anthem before classes started. And from first grade until the end of high school, we studied Peruvian history. Manco Capac, Sinchi Roca, Roca Yupanqui, Ayar Huaca! I can still recite the name of every Inca, every viceroy, and every president. How many Americans can do the same with their country's leaders?

The history of the War of the Pacific was taught very differently in Peruvian and Chilean schools. My father enjoyed asking his Chilean friends about it. To the Chileans, our hero Alfonso Ugarte was a coward who covered the head of his horse with the Peruvian flag and jumped into the ocean just before being taken prisoner. To us, Ugarte was a model of bravery who jumped into the ocean rather than risk having the flag of his country fall into enemy hands.

Politicians in both countries conveniently kept alive the possibility of another war as a way of distracting people's attention from other concerns, such as the constantly bad economic news or the droughts in the sierra or the floods in the Amazon. Headlines would appear in the paper: "Chile accuses Peru of buying thirty tanks and stationing them at its borders," or "Chilean Army headquarters at the Peruvian border doubles its capacity."

Tacna was forty miles from the Chilean town of Arica. The war created a tension between these two towns that never completely disappeared. To travel the forty miles that separated them was an exercise in endurance, so many visas and official papers were needed. Yet Tacna and Arica had a symbiotic relationship, living off each other's surpluses and shortages. A band of women known as *contrabandistas* traveled back and forth every day smuggling goods that one town had in abundance and the other one lacked. In the mornings they boarded the small train that linked the towns, their large bellies and breasts made of sugar, flour, or detergent. My father called this army of oddly shaped women "the rebel soldiers of the marketplace." Yet other than being a domestic or a market vendor, this was then one of the few occupations a woman could have. Father did not want Mother to buy the *contrabandistas'* goods, but often I saw Mother, who had little regard for convention, ignore his wishes. She did not bargain with them as she did with the vendors in the market, because she knew it was no use; they would not budge.

The *contrabandistas* were regarded as an eccentric, courageous group. Their bold life brought them a grudging kind of respect. Some of them even dressed in pants, a highly unusual practice for women at that time. They were classified in a special category, along with the other mysterious group of women in town, the mistresses, who also dressed loudly and were outspoken. In a small town like ours, we knew who these particular women were, and we were taught to look discreetly the other way when we passed one on the street. Occasionally one of the *contrabandistas* would get caught by the customs officers, but since the jail was set up only for men, they were released after a quick questioning. This was one of the few advantages my town conferred on women.

In the Peru of my youth, a woman who worked was an embarrassment to her family, a sign of their poverty. My father refused to have women work in his business, although he had a different reason: to him, women in the workplace were troublemakers. "The minute you hire a woman, it all becomes gossip," he would say very seriously. When I was young, I never questioned this, and years later, when I did, he chose not to reply.

The women of Tacna lived hard lives. Their youth was centered on the authoritarian figures of their fathers, who were at best benevolent dictators from whom they learned the fate that awaited them. Early in life, a woman was expected to work hard at getting a husband who would be a good match and improve her lot. Social mobility was not easy, and after marriage, a woman's husband's life became her own. For instance, there was the mother of my schoolmate Carmen Gomes.

Carmen lived not far from my house, and I often stopped to pick her up so we could walk to school together. On a small table in the center of her living room was a large picture of Señora Gomes in her wedding gown. I never got tired of looking at that picture, which dominated the room. She looked so beautiful with her black hair piled high on her head, framing her perfectly oval face. Her enormous dark eyes curved obliquely above high cheekbones. In her white lace wedding gown, she seemed wrapped in a cloud. I couldn't believe she was the same woman who greeted us when we came home from school: short and heavy, with her hair pulled back in a bun. She couldn't have been older than thirty-five, yet her looks and her desire to look good had evaporated. She was in constant motion, running to and from the market, turning her husband's shirt collars, dusting the furniture, watering the plants. The table with the photograph seemed to be a small altar, constructed to remind herself and her family of the beauty she had been.

At exactly twelve o'clock, everything changed in Carmen's normally roiling house. Suddenly it became calm and orderly, and Señor Gomes arrived for lunch. He would sit at the head of the table, a small, balding man with a very thin mustache, and ask his wife, "Dear, what are you spoiling me with today?" The poor woman broke into a sweat as she told him the menu, which consisted of several courses. Like most men in my town, Señor Gomes had a bureaucratic job in one of those places where typewriters had to be shared and supply requests sent to the capital. His tasks were menial and his salary modest. But at home he was treated like a minor lord. Señora Gomes had to perform miracles to stretch his meager salary. Carmen's father acted as if he were an important guest, and he expected all kinds of deference. He devoured his meal in somber silence, but if anything went wrong, he would break into a tempest. When he had managed to reduce everyone to tears, he would storm out of the house like a spoiled child, and sometimes not return for days.

Carmen's mother's life was not very different from that of any other woman in Tacna. Their only consolations were their children and each other's company. On Sundays after Mass they gathered together in the plaza and exchanged their woes, their recipes, and their home remedies.

Later I learned that Carmen's father, like so many men in my town, had what was called a "little house," where he kept his mistress and their illegitimate children. I now could solve the mystery of where he went when he disappeared, yet I wondered how he treated his mistress, if he treated his legitimate family so badly.

This way of life still exists in my country, but women like Carmen and her mother have fought tough, long battles so their daughters can go to the universities, where women now make up almost half of the student body. Painful silences are slowly being tolerated less.

10

THE HOUSE WHERE I GREW UP

THE HOUSE my parents built was a hybrid. Mother, who designed much of it herself, borrowed features from the vernacular architecture of Peru, from her native Italy, and from a collection of architecture books she had sent from Europe. The result was a large, comfortable house built around a central courtyard and situated in the middle of a carefully planned, harmonious garden. The house was built of adobe, which was covered with white stucco. It had dark green shutters and a red tile roof. It looked out toward the garden, which was an integral part of the space.

It is almost impossible to imagine the amount of work that went into putting the house together. The furniture was functional and modern, covered in bright colored cloth. The fabrics for the living room were specially dyed in the colors found in native weavings, and the rugs were woven to Mother's own designs. The tiles for the kitchen and bathrooms were made in Lima and became a popular attraction for visiting school-mates, who had never seen tilework. Ancient Peruvian pottery and weavings provided the accents.

The courtyard was filled with potted plants. Jasmine scented the air with a sweet smell, red and purple bougainvillea cast a soft hue, and cacti added an exotic touch. One of the cacti produced an enormous flower that opened for only a few hours each year. We chil-dren were allowed to stay up late to watch this flow-ering. In the middle of the courtyard was a huge bird-cage made of colonial ironwork and filled with yellow canaries. Seated in our little chairs, we watched atten-tively as the flower slowly opened and the canaries sang into the night.

The garden surrounding the house was organized so that from each window our atypical desert views con-sisted of a soothing range of greens: the delicate green of the olive trees, the sharp soft green of the grass, the dusty tired green of the tall pine trees, and the watery green of the grape arbors. In the front of the house, which was set back from the street, there were fruit trees: trees full of lemons, tender apricots, avocados, which Mother considered exotic, and oranges, whose blossoms were feasts to the delicate hummingbirds. We also had a large mulberry tree, which bore fruit for Mother's syrup, a culinary coup.

In the back and on the sides of the house were herb and vegetable gardens and rose gardens consisting of about a hundred different varieties. These were linked by paths and framed by beds of tender flowers such as jonquils, gerberas, sweet peas, and nasturtiums. At the back of the house stood the tall eucalyptus trees that seemed to guard our house like soldiers. How this garden grew with the little water that came through once every two weeks was a miracle of planning by Mother and her gardener, Pablo.

I still remember the rains of 1956. So much water came down that the gringo Cooper's plane could not land. For more than a week we were cut off from the world. When the rain stopped, the thin dust that was usually suspended in the desert air was gone, and everything shone with extraordinary vividness. The pale pink adobe walls of the houses turned a deep salmon shade, and the dusty palm trees glowed a brilliant green. The smell of wet adobe saturated the air with an unfamiliar earthiness, which mingled with the scent of jasmine. The wet ground felt unnaturally soft beneath our feet. Everything seemed refreshed.

A true miracle took place in the desert. The vast landscape, which had been barren and brown, was covered by a mantle of lavender-pink flowers. It was soft and lush, and every day for as long as the flowers lasted my parents took us to roll in them, just as my children later rolled in the soft just-fallen snow of the New England winter.

Ours was the only house in town the rain had not penetrated. I remember being embarrassed to tell my friends at school that our house remained dry. I made up a story about having spent the nights in the car. Rain became magical to me, a good omen, because it was during the rains that my parents informed me that I would be sent to where I would not have to tell lies to be like everyone else. I was being sent to London, where I wanted to go. There, among people whose language and customs I did not share, I would learn that I had to work very hard in other ways to be like everyone else.

The last time I saw my house was a year ago, when my sister and brother and I went back to Tacna to bury my mother. I walked through the garden with mixed emotions and confused memories. I realized that my intense feelings about this place had kept me company all my life. The childhood events that I remembered and those that were later told to me merged. The things that had seemed wonderful and exotic to a young person, like having the only grand piano in town, or the fifty-volume *Encyclopedia Espasa*, which had arrived in huge cases from Argentina, had become less significant. I caught a fleeting moment of childhood again as I recalled the old church bell that called us to lunch, the scent of orange blossoms mixed with the cologne that Mother used, the way the afternoon sun reflected on the white wall that surrounded the property, making it pink and soft, or the sound of a bird, so alive in my memory that it brought into focus even more remote memories, like a tiny flower unexpectedly found pressed into a book.

Now the house stands empty, waiting to be sold. In today's Peru these houses are too dangerous to live in, too exposed and vulnerable to terrorism. The garden is dry; only the most resilient plants are left. The scent of the flowers has been replaced by gas fumes from the traffic of a town that has grown too fast. Whereas once our house stood at the edge of town, it is now part of the center. The land that was the garden is too valuable to be a private garden, and it has been parceled out into a development. I dream that someone will buy the house and restore it, though I know this will not happen. The place as it was will continue only in my memories. Like my parents, who left their native Italy, my siblings and I left our home, seduced by America or by better opportunities in Lima.

Tacna has changed, too. The town is now a city, the population has mushroomed, and the government, in a desperate attempt to provide prosperity, has made Tacna a tax-free zone for foreign goods. Import taxes in the rest of Peru are enormous. Now a different kind of *contrabandista* comes to Tacna from elsewhere in Peru, not to exchange staples but to purchase VCRs, TVs, whiskey, and imported perfumes. The few general stores that provided us with all our needs have been replaced by sleek emporiums of the latest technologies. In the marketplaces where we did our daily shopping, the gentle Indian women who sold potatoes and herbs are gone. A beehive of vendors aggressively attack consumers with Taiwanese and Korean copies of Rolex watches and Chanel perfumes, imported canned foods and T-shirts.

Tacna, like so much of Peru, has also become a center for drugs. Living in such a despairing economic reality, in search of a livelihood, many people have turned to this highly profitable industry. Coca grows in the Andes, but it moves through border towns like Tacna on its way to its markets. The drugs have brought crime, and now people carefully lock their doors. Most of the families I knew growing up have moved away to Lima and other destinations to look for better opportunities. The gentle notes of a neighbor's piano at night have been replaced by the loud music of American hard rock. Columbus is still there, dustier, a forgotten hero, blamed for so much that went wrong.

11
MY PARENTS' DAY

ON THE SECOND DAY of June every year, they appeared exactly at noon: the bishop, the mayor, the headmasters of the schools, the captains from the local garrison, the dentists, the doctors, and the lawyers, *la crème de la crème* of our town. Perched on their arms came their wives. The men wore their finest suits; the women strapped themselves into girdles and sported the results of laborious sessions with their dressmakers and hairdressers.

My parents stood at the entrance to our living room and greeted their guests. I still remember the two of them standing by the door. My mother, dressed in a soft silk dress, moved as if she caressed the air around her. Her long brown hair was like a halo around her very pale face. For this occasion she made a special concession to makeup and wore dark pink lipstick. My father stood at her side, tall and erect, dressed in an elegant blue suit.

It was my parents' event. They were celebrating June 2, the Italian national holiday. Soon after they married, the Italian government made Father an honorary consul, a position of which he was immensely proud. In this official capacity, he invented this celebration with my mother. For a day, our house was the center of town. So important did this day become in Tacna that most businesses closed, just as they did for the Peruvian national holidays.

Early in the morning, the Italian flag rose from the mast in front of our house, and at noon my parents' guests came to enjoy what they viewed as an authentic Italian celebration. The preparations went on all year.

Months before the event, Father drove to Arica, the nearest harbor, and ordered from the captains of the Italian liners the most exquisite of Italian delicacies: prosciutto and Parmesan cheese, biscotti and Perugina chocolates, candied fruits and olive oil. The champagne and whiskey came by truck from Lima, and so did boxes of unusual fresh fruits and vegetables, such as passion fruit and white asparagus. The pantry bulged with supplies.

Two weeks before the day, the house was in a frenzy of activity. Mother, like a general in battle, commanded not only our regular servants but the extra help that was hired for the occasion. Fresh pasta was rolled, piles of cheese were grated, cakes were baked, silver was polished, flowers were arranged, floors were waxed. The maids wore special black uniforms for this event, with lace aprons, and the waiters wore gloves, as they did in Lima.

When everyone had arrived, Father read a short speech, while the rest of the family suffered in silence. He was a terrible public speaker, and although his writing was eloquent, his delivery was awful. Despite endless rehearsals, the speech never came out right. Sometimes he read the same line twice, or skipped one. Mother stood next to him stoically, waiting for it to end so that he could enjoy his party. Not long ago I found a copy of one of his speeches, a beautiful, poetic salute to Peru and to his friends there.

The festivities went on all day. The women discreetly gathered in the living room while the men stayed in the garden. The waiters never stopped passing food; the guests, especially the men, never stopped eating. As a child, I was always amazed at the gluttony of these men. Mother was continually approached by husbands who wanted her to teach their wives how to make these delicacies.

When it began to get dark, the wives got up their courage and en masse flowed from the house to the garden to fetch their husbands. This was the one uncomfortable moment of the day. "One more," the men would plead, as they stopped the waiters for an extra drink. The bishop, who had no wife, was always the last to leave.

Every year when the party was over, Mother told Father, "I will never do it again," but then, knowing how happy this day made him, she would. She did it for twenty-five years, until Father died.

I remember the year Father was able to get Gorgonzola cheese. The pungent smell permeated the kitchen. The guests ate very little of it, and later Saturnina informed us that some of them had commented that the butter was rancid this year. Gorgonzola disappeared from the menu forever. I also remember when I came back from my first year in college and Mother and I made pizza, an Italian dish best known in America. It was an enormous success, and I, too, felt proud to contribute to Father's pleasure.

Years later, on one of my trips to Peru, I ran into a

friend who had been a regular at our parties. He told me he had just returned from a holiday in Italy. "I wanted to see for myself the country whose customs I experienced so joyfully every June," he said. If only he had been able to say this to my parents.

12

THE GRINGO COOPER

IN THE TACNA of my youth, our main contact with the outside world came every day more or less at noon with the arrival of the tiny orange mail plane of the gringo Cooper. My father and I drove over to the airstrip after lunch to wait for him to land with the mail. While we waited we played a game: whoever could spot the plane first would win. There was a penalty if either of us confused it with a bird. To let me win, my father sometimes pretended to look in the wrong direction.

The appearance of the plane seemed a sort of miracle to me. It would first be visible as a tiny spot between the low hills not far from the airfield. As the black spot turned orange, the noise of the engine filled the quiet desert, and soon the plane bounced down the cleared patch of sand that was the runway, leaving a brown cloud behind it. When the dust settled, the door opened and the gringo Cooper emerged.

Philip Arthur Cooper was a tall blond man. His legs were long and straight. His deep-set blue eyes seemed almost transparent against his tanned skin. He was an expatriate Englishman, an adventurer who shared the skies of Peru with the condors. The gringo Cooper was the romantic hero of my youth. I never tired of admiring this tall, gruff man who barely spoke Spanish and liked to pat everyone on the back. Not only did Cooper bring us the news of the world, but every important person who visited our town arrived with him. When the Americans came to work in the copper mines, they arrived one by one with the gringo Cooper; when the cardinal of Peru came for a visit, it was the gringo Cooper who helped him out of the plane (the long red robes that covered his large body made it hard for him to do it with dignity).

One day the gringo Cooper offered to take me and Father for a ride. I sat on Father's lap. He said something to me, but I could not hear him above the roar of the engine. The plane took off slowly and rose into the air. I floated along, scared to death. Suddenly we dove, going down and still farther down in a seemingly endless dive. My stomach sickened; my hands clung to my father's. Just as suddenly we went up again, victorious, into the sky. The two grownups were laughing.

I closed my eyes and did not open them again until we landed.

As I got out of the plane, I let out a huge sigh. "We almost fell out of the sky," I mustered my courage to say.

Cooper laughed and shook his head. In his awkward Spanish, he said, "We just bowed to your mother. Did you see her waving in the garden?"

"Yes," I lied.

My father knew better but said nothing.

Occasionally Father would persuade the gringo Cooper to come to our house. The two of them sat under Father's favorite tree and exchanged stories. I can almost see them, bigger than life, two strong men triumphant in their adventures: my father settled, with a family, a house, and a place of business, the gringo Cooper always moving, his place of business the sky, his office his tiny plane, or "the orange horse," as Father called it.

Cooper had come to Peru as a pilot for the English company that built the railroads. He fell under Peru's spell and stayed all his life. He had set himself to discover the most remote parts of the country, to fly above the Andes and the Amazon. His planes got bigger and bigger, and eventually he started his own airline.

For many years after my childhood I did not see him. I just saw his planes at the Lima airport, with his name in bright orange letters. He and Father remained friends, and when Father died, the gringo Cooper came to visit us. Mother and I were sitting in the garden when we spotted Saturnina following a thin figure dressed in white and sporting a wide-brimmed hat. He moved slowly toward us, still tall and straight, his debonair outfit failing to hide how much he had aged. His face was a confusion of wrinkles, his blue eyes oases of clarity. He drank his whiskey as fast as always, but he seemed restless, as if he had something to tell us. Cooper asked Mother if he could speak to me in English, and then, slowly, he told me his love story.

"It might seem odd to you that I want to tell you the story of my Lola, the woman I married. I want you to know it because your father was as close as I came to having a family. We were brothers in adventure. When he was young, before he married, we flew together to places no one had been before. We discovered rivers and lakes not even the natives had seen. We flew over mountains covered in omnipresent snow and landed on uncharted land where there were only a few llamas to greet us.

"Later, after you were born, the happiest moment of my day was the sight of you and your father waiting for me to land. You were so shy, holding your father's hand, with those long braids of yours, and those curious eyes. Your father and I could do no wrong in your eyes. I had a lot to do with your life, even if you don't know it. It was I who persuaded your parents to send you to England instead of to Switzerland to school, as they wanted. What good have the Swiss ever done? They lack imagination and traditions. We English have a queen and a great history. Secretly, I wanted you to learn my language, so that when I got old, as I am now, I could talk to you. I lost you, too, just as your parents did. You fell in love with the places you visited, and you made your life somewhere else. I guess the blood of adventurers does not die easily."

A long silence followed. I felt that it was hard for him to tell me about Lola, so I asked him to do so.

"You never met her, but your father did. He liked her. Lola has been my woman and my friend for many years. I met her in Iquitos. She was the daughter of the owners of the little pension where I stayed. Lola is my tall, dark, strong Amazonian beauty, one hundred per-cent Peruvian, like the Andes and the Incas. She gave me my only child. Sadly, my daughter died at birth. It was your father who helped me get Lola to a good doctor in Lima, or I would have lost her, too. Lola never asked anything of me, except that she always wanted me to take her to England. She wanted to meet my family. I have no family, so I married her and told her that she was my family. For years she waited for me in Iquitos. I did not get there often. She understood that my life was crossing the skies, yet there she created a home for me and gave me much happiness. Three years ago I had a stroke. I could not fly anymore. I moved to Iquitos and sold the airline. Now I just think about my airplanes, like a flock of birds in the sky."

That was the last time I saw the gringo Cooper. He died shortly thereafter. Mother called to tell me. She sounded very sad. "He was the last of that generation," she said, "so much like your father. There are no more like them." Mother sent me his obituaries, which were written in heroic terms. Cooper was called "the father of Peruvian aviation," "a model entrepreneur," "the indomitable Englishman." Our local paper called him "the English condor," which is the way I like to think of him, a hero who made me bow to my mother from the sky, who crossed virgin skies to visit places not even the condors could reach. Like my father, he was a brave man who left a strong mark on his adopted country. Later Mother told me that Lola went on a trip to England. She wanted to discover for herself the country of the man she loved.

13
A PORCELAIN DOLL

THERE WERE THOSE who came to Peru and remained untouched; in their thoughts and surroundings, they remained as faithful as they could to the place they had left behind. They created lives that were like small islands, isolated, filled with nostalgia, deprived of the excitement of the new. They chose not to return to their original countries, for their departures had been final separations, but as the years went by and they failed to connect, their situations became more extreme. To us children, they embodied a different kind of mystery: exotic specimens from worlds we longed to know.

One such person was Madame Bandol. She arrived from France with her husband, an architect who came to build the Eiffel cathedral. They were recently married and brought their furniture, their silver and china, and her piano. They moved into a little house near the plaza. He, I was told, was incredibly handsome, tall, full of the kind of arrogance good-looking Europeans were meant to have. He came from a distinguished French family and had married beneath his class. His family refused to accept his wife, so he took a job in Peru and they set off for the unknown. She was a small, fragile woman, with skin so fair it was almost transparent. She spoke no Spanish, and devoted her life only to him. Every evening they would walk arm in arm along the *alameda*, and afterward she would play her small upright piano until late at night. At that time it was the only piano in our town. People left their windows open so that they could hear her music in the peace of the night. Otherwise, she never went out.

In the morning, her maid went to the market and bought strange foods such as fish roe and rooster combs.

My friend Ana told me that her father made a special detour on his way home for lunch so that he could smell the scents that came from her kitchen. They reminded him of the year he had spent in Paris as a young man. Mother told me that she and Father paid the Bandols a courtesy call when they arrived, and that Madame Bandol was gracious and charming but also shy and distant.

One day shortly after they arrived, Monsieur Bandol died of a heart attack. He died so quickly there was not even time to get a doctor. The whole town showed up for his funeral. Madame Bandol walked behind the coffin with a black veil covering her face. In those days women did not attend funerals, but everyone understood this exception. After the funeral, when it was customary for the townswomen to visit the widow, the maid stood at the door and told people her *patrona* wished to be left alone. Late into that night she played the piano, music so sad that people closed their windows.

After that, she never left the house again. Many nights I went to sleep to the sad notes of her piano. Every Tuesday, Mother went to have tea with her, and sometimes she would take me along. I remember everything about her: her tiny figure, her face covered with white powder, her thin blond hair piled on top of her head like a crown. She always dressed in white. The only touches of color were the large pink satin bows on her shoes. Her exotic scent still lingers in my mind; Mother told me it was a perfume called Mitsouko. Madame Bandol looked to me like one of the porcelain dolls she kept in a cabinet next to the chair where I was always instructed to sit.

She and Mother spoke in French. I did not mind, because there were so many things to look at in her crowded, lavender-tinted living room: photographs of elegant people in ivory frames, lamps made of shimmering crystal, with silk shades; oddly shaped soft pillows; tiny silver dishes filled with candies; lace curtains and gilded chairs. For tea she served tiny cakes, so small you needed two to make a real bite. She thought I was too young to have tea, so the maid gave me lemonade, which was bitter. She always told Mother to remind me to watch my posture. "A woman can never be really beautiful if she doesn't have good posture," she would say.

After tea, she played the piano. She could play only certain things, because her hands were so small. She cried as she played; sometimes Mother did, too. When it was time to leave, she gave me a marron glacé. Once she gave me a lace parasol. Her maid would follow us home to carry the magazines she was returning to Mother and to pick up new ones.

Mother tried to get her to teach French, to give piano lessons. Nothing appealed to her. She wouldn't even come to our house for tea. Mother just helped her as best she could. When her maids quit, which they often did because her house was such a sad place to work, Mother would send Saturnina to help until she found a new maid for her. Saturnina told me that Madame Bandol spent the day writing in a little leather book and reading Mother's magazines. She also said that at night the soul of Madame Bandol's husband came to keep her company. Saturnina had seen a tall figure of a man standing by the piano while Madame Bandol played. When Saturnina walked into the room, the figure disappeared, because the souls of the dead are visible only to the ones they love.

Mother and I visited Madame Bandol on my vacations home from college in America. Nothing ever changed. Her place looked a little smaller and a little more faded as the years went by. Mother was always kind to her, though she stopped dreaming up projects for her.

One day when I returned on vacation, Mother told me that Madame Bandol had died. "She was everything I am not," Mother said. "She was so loyal to her customs. Her house was a little island of France. Mine has so little of Italy." I couldn't quite understand what Mother meant by that. Now I understand it well. I, too, often look at my house and my life in America and feel a sense of disloyalty about what I have abandoned of my past in Peru.

When I asked Mother what happened to Madame

Bandol's furniture and piano, she said, "Nicolette stipu-
lated in her will that her remains should be sent to
France. Everything she owned will go to an orphanage
there, too." It was the first time Mother referred to her
by her first name. When I took my children to Peru,
they wanted to see the French house where I had had
tea when I was young. There was nothing left, just the
memories of the sound of Madame Bandol's piano.

14

OUR HOUSE AT THE BEACH

OUR LITTLE BEACH HOUSE stood alone, minus-
cule in the immensity of the Pacific coast. It was Mother's
idea that we build a beach house. Unlike the other
people of my town, whose roots drew them to the
earth, my parents had the ocean at the center of their
lives. On the beach they could watch the endless waves,
as they had as children. The adventures of Genoese
sailors had inspired Father's youthful dreams, and the
ocean had brought them to Peru. Now the ocean was
an enormous blue space that separated them from their
families. The beach house became a place all our own,
because no one else in our town ever went there.

There, I assumed, we did things the way they were done in my parents' country, things that became so sacred to me I never shared them with my schoolmates, like cooking octopus on a grill, or swimming with our clothes off, or eating raw sea urchins.

Every Sunday very early in the morning, Saturnina and the maids packed up Father's convertible and our little family left. There was no road, just the track that our car followed, leaving clouds of sand behind. The desert's monotonous brownness was disturbed by an occasional mirage, which vanished almost as quickly as it had appeared. Father drove fast, and Mother sang Italian songs, some that she had known as a child, others that Father had taught her. The trip took an hour. We could tell we were almost there when we heard the restless waves in the distance. The noise persisted and grew louder and louder, until we could no longer hear Mother's singing. Suddenly the vast blue sea would appear, its endless movement in stark contrast to the calm of the desert. The color of the sand changed from the dry sand of the desert to the wet sand of the beach.

We all rushed to open the house. It was made of wood and filled with large windows that let in the breezes. It consisted of a single enormous room. With only a tiny kitchen in one corner, we did our cooking outside on the grill or brought our food already prepared. The rest of the room was sparsely furnished with large, comfortable wicker chairs and couches covered in blue-and-white-striped fabric. Pillows of various colors and shapes were scattered all over. We ate at a long table on the terrace, which was as large as the house.

The day moved to our self-imposed rituals. The morning was for walking on the beach or for fishing. Some Sundays we walked to a beach we called "the Beach of the Phantoms," because from there we could see a small island where sea lions lived. What a haunting apparition they made! Their large, amorphous brown bodies moved awkwardly; their mournful laments sent a wave of fear through my body. Occasionally we would find one of their big tusks washed up on the beach. I once gave one to Saturnina. She had never heard of sea lions, but she told me it was the tooth of a devil embodied in an animal. In order to disperse its evil, she washed it in vinegar and wrapped it in rue before she threw it away.

The food we had for lunch at the beach was different from anything we ate at home. It consisted mostly of a variety of cold dishes: artichoke frittata, tomatoes stuffed with corn and clams, shredded arugula salad, marinated baby eggplants, anchovies in a bed of sweet peppers, cold turkey breast in a tuna and caper sauce, and for dessert, cold fried rice with molasses and raisin sauce, or fresh fruit salad, the fruit cut in pieces so small that each ingredient became almost indistinguishable.

After the long lunch, which changed every Sunday but was always delicious, we spent the afternoon reading. Mother picked the material according to our ages and according to the courses we needed help with at school. We were also allowed to read one comic book each. Mother always read the same book, *The Divine Comedy*; it was to Italians what *Don Quixote* was to the Spanish. It seemed such a mysterious book to me. My first year in college I signed up for a course on *The Divine Comedy*, and I soon understood why Mother never got tired of reading it.

Father brought his newspapers, but sometimes as we sat in our reading corners, I could hear Mother's voice reading to Father. Then I would sneak up and sit behind her chair to listen. Father pretended not to see me. As the sun began to set, it was our turn to have Mother read to us. She had a big fat book she had bought in Lima called *Our Universe*. From it, we learned about galaxies, planets, rivers in Africa, and Eskimos in Alaska.

We waited until the sun went down before we rushed to pack the car and return home. We had to be very quiet in the car so that Father could find the way back in the dark. A few times, on nights when there was no moonlight, we got lost. We could hear the night animals in the distance, wild mules and wolves, their long, lonely calls emerging from the otherwise empty land. But there, when I was together with my family, fear did not exist.

15

LIMA, THEN AND NOW

THE LIMA I KNEW when I was growing up was a garden city of calm and discreet elegance, which those of us who lived in the provinces would visit from time to time. Going to Lima was like making a pilgrimage to a splendorous haven. We flew above the long, dry Peruvian desert in a small airplane whose roaring engine interrupted the still silence of the big blue sky. From the window we could see an occasional tiny river fighting its way down from the Andes, a small oasis of green beside it.

As we neared Lima, the plane became enveloped in clouds. Regardless of the season or time of day, Lima is always wrapped in a gray cover. The Limenos call it *neblina*, a cloud of mist that hangs over the city and makes it moist and mysterious. It is said that, to curse the Spanish conquistadors, the Indians suggested this location for the capital of the viceroyalty. After all, the rest of the coast of Peru has clear and open skies. Through the years, as I have returned to Lima, other curses have haunted this city, and the grayness of the fog has become an emblem of its moods.

The little plane dove through the fog. For a short while even the wings seemed to disappear, until we landed with a glorious bounce. The airport terminal in those days was a small white building. From the plane's window I could see the *interamericanos*, the Panagra planes, which were the symbol of modernity. These DC-4s were small compared to the 747s that now fly to Lima, yet when I was a child they appeared enormous. I would admire the people who streamed in and out of them and imagine that they were traveling to the places in Mother's magazines, like New York and Paris. I said secret prayers that I would someday go there, too.

After disembarking and gathering our bags, we took a taxi, something we did not have in our town, to our hotel. Lima was then a calm city that marched to muzzled rhythms. We passed low white structures on wide streets framed by jacaranda trees, which tinged the air with a soft blue cast. Great colonial houses still stood in the center of town, their carved wooden balconies as delicate as lace. From these high perches women watched the daily routines of the city unfold. These women were modern versions of the *tapadas*, women in colonial times who covered half their faces with veils in an adaptation of Moorish customs that came to us when Spain sent viceroys to Peru. These early emissaries built big, drafty houses for their families, with huge courtyards, whitewashed walls, and roofs made of mud. An architecture that mixed the Spanish and the native, its charm resided in its odd use of materials. Like the houses in which they lived, the women led lives that were a peculiar mixture of imported customs and native ones.

In downtown Lima, the most cosmopolitan and sophisticated street was the Jirón de la Union, where we would admire the smartly dressed people and shop for the latest styles. It was a gentle street where men practiced what an Italian friend of mine used to call "a most Peruvian form of art." The *piropo* is a verbal flattery, half serious, half mocking, that men on the street whisper to women. It was on the Jirón de la Union where I heard my first: "*Madrecita*, where you step, jasmine will grow." I laughed, only to be reprimanded by my mother. "You are supposed to blush, not laugh," she said. When my mother got one — "With such a good-looking mother, God only knows what the daughter will turn out to be" — I noticed that she blushed, but also that she smiled. When we went home and I told my father about it, he said he would come to protect us the next day. Of course he did not. He knew that we had both enjoyed our *piropos*.

At school when we were older we exchanged men's *piropos* the way my children did baseball cards. Some girls recorded them in special little books. My daughter and I laugh together over the irony inherent in a situation so innocent. Whereas this attention from men was a form of flattery we then enjoyed, today in the United States it would be interpreted as a kind of sexual harassment.

As *provincianos*, we could be spotted immediately, since we always looked slightly out of step. A friend of my mother's refused ever to go to Lima, claiming she got dizzy from all the activity — a possibility now that Tacna has 200,000 inhabitants and Lima almost 2 million, but hard to imagine thirty-five years ago, when my town had a population of 35,000 and Lima only half a million. As a child I longed for my trips to Lima, to visit the fancy shops with my mother and buy dresses that I could show off to my friends at home, or to go to the big moviehouses to see foreign stars like Esther Williams in *Neptune's Daughter.* At the only moviehouse in Tacna they showed chiefly Mexican movies, which I was not allowed to see because there was too much kissing.

What I liked best in Lima was staying at the Hotel Bolívar. There was so much there that was new and exotic to me. It was the first building I had ever been in that had more than two floors and a little room that moved up and down, called an elevator. The Bolívar was at the center of Lima, in Plaza San Martín, an enormous square filled with activity. Unlike the plaza in my town, where people went only on Sundays or national holidays, here the movement never stopped. At night I could see the lights of the neon signs: the Coca-Cola one went on and off in different patterns, and the large Phoenix Insurance Company bird raised and lowered its wings.

The Bolívar was filled with foreign tourists and *provin-*

cianos like us. The tourists, mostly French and American, spoke very little Spanish, and usually sat at the bar drinking pisco sours as they waited for their guides to take them to see the city or for the weather to clear so they could fly to Cuzco. The Americans spoke in loud voices and wore blue jeans and pointy boots. They didn't eat lunch in the dining room as we did, but would order strange things called sandwiches, two slices of bread with meat and cheese in between. I would have given anything to try one, but it seemed improper even to ask.

The waiters were always hovering around the Americans, because they tipped constantly. I was intimidated by them. Although they were called gringos, as we were, they appeared very different to me. I couldn't figure out what we had in common except our pale skins. They brazenly broke the rules of public behavior we had so carefully been taught, such as saying "good morning" when you entered the elevator and addressing strangers formally. We were very much the discreet *provincianos*, who wore city clothes and had a drink only in the evening, before dinner.

My father knew all the other *provincianos*, and he often had business meetings with them to discuss the price of cotton and politics. I ate with their children in the children's dining room, where we were allowed to order our own meals. How sophisticated I felt, choosing my own food.

Coming from the provinces, where our families were different from most of the local people, we were small-town versions of Lima's *oligarcas,* or rich people. We felt bonded. Our favorite form of conversation was to exchange exaggerated stories about our lives in the provinces. I still remember Salomon, the boy from Trujillo who told me that his parents were so rich they sent their French linens back to France to be laundered so the impure water of Peru would not turn them yellow; and Magdalena, from Ica, who told me that for her sister's wedding her family built a chapel with an altar made of gold.

Another favorite topic was the schools our parents would be sending us to when we reached the right age. It was customary to send daughters to a year of finishing school, usually in Switzerland, and sons to agricultural or engineering colleges in the United States. I remember how I admired my friends' oldest siblings, who would come back from these schools for vacations. They were promoted to the grownups' dining rooms and dressed in the latest styles. They would show off their English and strike up conversations with the tourists. They also told us about American girls who weren't virgins, and how much more fun Americans were than Latinas. Of course, I was not exactly sure what being a virgin meant. I just listened, waiting eagerly for my turn to plunge into that sophisticated world.

How sheltered we were, shielded not only from the news of the world, which would later come to us on TV, but from the world of the adults we lived with. Like delicate plants, we were kept in greenhouses, our growth carefully monitored and regulated by strict cultural rituals. The Hotel Bolívar was just a tiny window on the world, and it made us curious for more.

The Lima of my youth was a city where the privileged lived lives of fantasy and detachment, far more extravagant than the lives of any *provincianos.* Fortunes were made from minerals, rubber, fishmeal, and guano, of such magnitude it is hard to comprehend how they came from a country so small. The *oligarcas* lived in mansions and on plantations in between their trips to Paris, where they bought their wines and acquired a taste for French literature. On our parents' trips to Lima, they were invited to the *oligarcas'* parties. Mother told us about Lima society ladies who spoke only French at teatime, wore clothes by the most elegant Parisian designers, and filled their houses with gilded mirrors, oriental carpets, fantastic collections of pre-Columbian art, and waiters in tails. "Little Versailles" is how Mother referred to their world.

Today Peru has a new set of oligarchs: the "coca lords," with their high-security mansions equipped with VCRs, movie screens, and other artifacts of the newest technologies. They spend little of their lives in Peru. For security and financial reasons they flock to Miami, where they live in condominiums, drive Mercedes Benzes, and dress in blue jeans.

Peru's resources are still mostly untapped. When Mother arrived in Peru, it was cheaper to buy serving trays made of silver than of china, so much silver came from Peru's mines. So amazingly rich was the country that the expression "Vale un Perú" ("It is worth Peru") is now used in Spanish-speaking countries to describe extraordinary wealth. Yet these resources stagnate, lost to bureaucracy, corruption, and lack of capital. Consider the story of the fishmeal industry. For years the rich waters of the Pacific provided Peru with this thriving business. In the early mornings, when we flew into Lima on the Braniff planes that succeeded Panagra's, we were greeted with a heavy sour smell that permeated the air. My family called it "the smell of dollars," a reference to the windfall of dollars brought to the country by the export of fishmeal. Yet during a strong leftist military dictatorship, the factories were nationalized. In the hands of inefficient and irresponsible government employees, fishing took place during the spawning season. Now the reassuring smell is gone, along with the fish. There are many other tales like this, of abundance turned into shortage. It is almost as if Peru is living what Saturnina called a curse.

Modernity came very slowly to the Peru of my youth. Every small step of its arrival became a memorable event: the first elevator, the first television, the first electric toaster. Like gifts from the American gods of progress, these novelties rattled our lives, and we accepted them with suspicious enthusiasm. At home Saturnina refused to use the electric toaster, claiming that it had a ghost inside it. Some of Mother's old friends still don't use elevators.

Those were days when soot and pollution did not yet cover the buildings like thick cobwebs; the years before terrorism and poverty forced people to encircle their homes with tall walls, depriving the city of its face; the years before Lima's gardens became unkempt and garbage gathered, uncollected, in streetcorners as food for stray dogs; the years before the population exploded and the city expanded into the "young towns," where families live in cardboard houses with tin roofs and no running water. Lima was then a safe place, where houses remained unlocked — something hard to understand, given the inequalities that always existed. I ask myself now what has happened as I walk through the streets of the city and experience the devastation caused by terrorism. It is as if Peru has burst apart, as if its reality became so awful that its people were forced to violent self-destruction.

On the corners where street poets used to dispense *piropos*, now young men with pocket calculators peddle dollars for Peruvian money. Peru has seen inflation of up to 2,700 percent a year, so while the poor rush to spend their wages, the more affluent convert them into dollars. The fancy stores have been supplanted by street peddlers known as *ambulantes*, who sell everything you can think of on the street. Pickpockets are also abundant; instead of enjoying an innocent *piropo*, you have to guard your pocketbook and hide your jewelry. The faces of the Limeños are sad, defiant, and speak of the fragility of their lives and of their fear for the future. How the faces of my people have changed in such a short time!

A friend and I walk through the streets of Miraflores, one of Lima's most exclusive neighborhoods. A blown-up building looms high above the crowded center, silent like a ghost, its inhabitants gone. Someone has placed a Peruvian flag on its roof; someone else has written VIVA EL PERÚ on one of its walls. Is this a statement of defiance or optimism?

Later we lock ourselves into our car and drive to a friend's house. The car is purposely old and nondescript so it will not attract attention. My friend doesn't say anything but waits for my reaction. I am silent too, for the truth that surrounds me is eloquent. We pass through a microcosm of today's Peru: security guards stationed at every corner and at the front doors of the more affluent houses, small children begging, people in line to get into buses, in line in front of government offices, in line at hospitals. We pass McDonalds restaurants and Pizza Huts, their garish colors already tired-looking from the soot. Street vendors prepare Peruvian food and offer for sale everything from Seiko watches and disposable diapers to peaches, medicinal herbs, and dollars. Sides of buildings are covered with political posters; bank offices are jammed next to repair shops and nightclubs. Under its dusty cover, the city pulses with a sense of desperation.

We arrive at our destination, a green oasis circled by tall fences and security guards. It is a hot day, and from the airy rooms of the house I can see the slums in the distance, sweating dust. There families are sharing a single source of water and patiently waiting with their skimpy buckets for their daily ration.

The conversation seems abstract to me, given the shantytowns that loom in the background. Yet I know my friends are not indifferent. With the characteristic optimism of Peruvians, they rest their hopes in politics, a national obsession. Peruvians of all classes fantasize that a new government will change things. This particular day is only six months before the presidential election. Everyone talks about Mario Vargas Llosa, the writer, as the undisputed winner. They hope that his international standing, his eloquence, and his sense of justice will set Peru on the right course.

Six months later I return to Peru. The new president is a man whose name was never mentioned that day at lunch, a second-generation Japanese Peruvian named Alberto Fujimori. I have yet to hear a credible explanation of what turned the tide. Most likely, Fujimori was simply a better salesman of hope.

16

DREAMING AMERICA

As a child, I used to watch the brilliant red sun as it disappeared over the horizon at our beach house and took the day away from us. Mother, who was seldom superstitious, told me that when the last sliver of the sun was about to disappear, we could make a wish. My wish was always the same: I wanted to go to the United States. There on the empty beach veiled in the pink tones of the desert sunset, I worked at inventing my version of America.

Much of my information about the United States came from Mother's magazines. They were my window onto the big, glamorous world so distant from my little town of Tacna. In *National Geographic* I saw the jungle of buildings in Manhattan, including the Chrysler Building, the most fanciful of all, its top radiating promise like a silver wedding cake piercing the sky. I saw the American desert, so different from my own, dotted with cacti. I learned about the miracle of the changing seasons: the leaves that turned radiant colors in the fall and then fell, the trees that appeared so dead in winter, then came alive in the spring. Through *House and Garden* I came to know the American suburban homes, so free and relaxed, their kitchens white, modern, and efficient. From *Vogue* I developed my idea of the way women dressed in America, their clothes chosen from enormous department stores with exotic names like Bloomingdale's and Lord & Taylor. Our dresses were dressmakers' copies of what we saw in magazines, disappointing finales to endless fittings. In a curious magazine called *The Ford Times*, I saw the variety of American cars. I imagined myself in a baby-blue convertible, driving across the Brooklyn Bridge.

I also saw pictures of American colleges, with their sprawling lawns and couples sitting unchaperoned under ancient trees. Even American foods seemed exotic to me — banana splits, cherries jubilee. On the Voice of America, I heard jazz. I assumed that its nervous, exciting tempo was that of life in America. Everything about the United States was miraculous to me. Friends went there on the verge of death and returned cured. American technology turned our arid desert into rich mines filled with copper. Americans' vast yellow earth-moving machines were like giants that took over both lanes of our newly built superhighway. The American president, a man named Eisenhower, seemed so kind and honest compared with our pompous politicians, who were always getting caught in scandals. My parents' friends thought it was the greatest joke that Americans made a fuss over a vicuña coat that the president's aide had accepted as a gift. We once had a president who was reputed to have left the country with the entire budget for the navy in his briefcase. As a young woman, I was at home the day the mayor's wife visited and suggested that my mother's silver tea set was something she would very much like to have. It was no coincidence that at that time my father was trying to get some licenses from City Hall.

Dreaming about America was a common occupation at school; after boys, America was the most popular topic. Mother's magazines came in handy. I developed a system of trading them for the *photonovelas* my friends had, which I was not allowed to read — fertile source material to me in inventing my own romances. I was amazed that I was never caught and was shocked when Mother told me years later that she knew about my scheme all along. Even Father, who felt women had no place in the world of business, thought this kind of trading showed some business acumen.

However, when the magazines were put away, life went back to the daily routines of a small provincial town where our parents had the power to control our knowledge and our thoughts, something unimaginable today. We met virtually no one outside our circle of friends who could challenge what we were told. One day the local paper wrote about a movie star who committed suicide. When we asked what suicide was, we were told that it was what people do when they have too many husbands, or when they show their bodies naked in public, or when they drink too much.

I still have friends in Peru who tell their children these moralistic white lies, just as Señorita Luisa did when she read my fortune in the wax.

I will always remember the first time I heard about homosexuality. Juanito, a schoolteacher in town, was found dead, his body next to that of a male stranger from another town. The news spread through town too fast for our parents to censor it. My friends' imaginations went wild. Some believed that Juanito was an unnatural phenomenon, born a man from the waist up and a woman from the waist down. Others maintained that he had been possessed by a devil who had turned him into a woman in the body of a man. The nuns told us that he was the devil because he had taken his own life, which was something that didn't belong to him but to God. They said that he had lost his self-discipline and that we should pray that people like him would not be born into our families. The maids in the kitchen blamed it all on the fact that he had never eaten the kind of roots that promote masculinity. We heard that the bishop refused to give the lovers a Catholic burial and they had to be buried in a part of the cemetery reserved for heathens. My mother simply told me that I was too young to know certain things, but that I shouldn't condemn Juanito and the other man.

The novelty finally wore off, but we never quite found out what a homosexual was. I have friends in Peru who still find it difficult to explain these "delicate subjects" to their children. My friend Ana tells me, "I would tell them, but my husband won't allow me to." She blushes when I say to her that I have very good friends who are homosexuals. How different Ana's world is from the world my children live in, where they can turn on the TV, watch a homosexual love scene, and understand what it is all about.

17
ITALY

I STILL REMEMBER the *Amerigo Vespucci*, a large white ocean liner, docked in the harbor at Arica, waiting to take me on my first trip to Italy. I was fourteen years old and completely absorbed in my preparations for this journey. The boat had appeared on the horizon early one morning, a floating fortress that was going to take me to explore the country that made me different from my classmates and that had given me so many small pleasures, such as inventing stories about relatives I had never seen and speaking in a language no one understood. I was finally going to see it all for myself.

Our family crossed what seemed to be an infinite

ocean, traveling in reverse the route my parents had taken years before. We went up the Peruvian coast, monotonous and brown. We stopped at harbors at all hours, in places we never bothered to wake up to see. One glorious noon we went through the Panama Canal and reached the Atlantic Ocean. We sailed on, surrounded by the blue ocean and the blue sky, a uniformity broken only at night by the star-sprinkled sky and a moon that got smaller bit by bit as we headed east.

After twenty-seven days at sea, we reached Italy. From the distance, in the bright afternoon light, the Ligurian coast was a succession of green hills dotted with what seemed like tiny grains of rice. As we got closer to Genoa, the landscape changed. Genoa clung to the mountains, stark and severe. The landmarks we knew so well from Mother's descriptions began to unveil their real selves. Some were taller or shorter, some bigger or smaller, and some were just as we had imagined them to be.

We navigated our way through a queue of cousins and relatives who had come to greet us. They were so many that I could not tell them apart. I just let them all hug me as our bags were packed into their tiny cars. Our procession moved slowly down a narrow road that seemed to be a succession of small tunnels. As we emerged from each tunnel, the view was that of the picture postcards that had arrived in the gringo Cooper's plane: tiny churches perched on top of green hills or at the edge of the Mediterranean; white villas surrounded by pine trees with tall trunks and sprawling, lazy tops; grand hotels built with turn-of-the-century elegance; cafés where old men drank their morning espresso, telling each other stories and eyeing the young women on the way to the beach; tiny rowboats gently bobbing in the calm sea; large sailboats playing games with the wind; shimmering white clouds echoing the white sails. Everything was wrapped in the sweet scent of oleanders and pines. How beautiful it seemed to me, how manicured and perfect. The rawness and emptiness of Peru was replaced by a warm, balanced density.

Our first visit was to Mother's mother. We arrived in the late afternoon. The lonely house looked ghostly in the twilight, foreboding and secretive. We had been told that it was going to be a difficult visit. My grandmother was very old, and we were cautioned to be kind. The gate was open and we let ourselves in. The garden was overgrown and smelled of dry earth. From close by, I could see that the paint on the house was peeling. We followed the only light that was on and came to the large living room. At the far end of the room sat my grandmother. In my imagination I expected a beautiful woman. What I found was a very old, fragile one, dressed in a faded violet silk kimono. Her hair was white, and she had little of it left. The lipstick she had put on did not follow the contour of her lips. She stared at us, and when Mother got closer, she said loudly, "Make sure you get some new clothes before you are seen in town. You look like rich South Americans." My heart went out to Mother. I knew how carefully she had planned what we would wear. I knew how she had longed for this visit.

The room smelled as if it had had no fresh air for a long time. Everything in it was as tired as the smell. The furniture, upholstered in black and purple velvet, was faded, the lace curtains had rips, and the flowers on top of the large piano were dusty and dried out. It was a short visit. Father sat close to Mother and tried to make conversation. The old lady did not answer. Mother sat very straight, like a little girl who has been told to behave. I know she was controlling her urge to cry. Finally we got up to leave. When we approached my grandmother to say goodbye, she handed each of us a package. Inside each, in an elaborate silver frame, was a picture of herself as a young woman: voluptuous, beautiful, and elegant. As we left the room I heard her say, "Remember me that way. I was not always the way I am now."

That was the only time I saw her. I know that Father and Mother went back again during our visit. They wanted her to have a maid, to move to a smaller, cozier place. She refused, and died there a year later. I wished that instead of my grandmother, I had met the mother superior who had raised Mother.

My grandmother was the only relative Mother had.

Everyone else we met came from Father's side of the family. At lunch the next day, in the large house where my father's family had lived for so many generations, I listened to my relatives, who all talked at once. People I had never seen knew everything about me, and proudly showed me an album they had made with pictures Mother had sent them. I looked around at the old pieces of furniture, guardians of my family's secrets. I tried to picture my father as a young man, doing his homework at a small desk in what had been his bedroom, or having his meals at the family table, which looked too short for his long legs to fit under. I watched the rain. How odd to see such vast quantities of water coming out of the sky.

We spent two weeks visiting relatives. These people, who were so exotic to me from the distance of Peru, started to become more real. Through the eyes of a fourteen-year-old, I observed that their lives were made up of routines that had not changed for generations, that their futures were predictably linked to their families' past. It was so unlike our life in Peru, which was continually being invented by my parents. Whereas my relatives kept curtains and furniture untouched, never questioning their color or place, everything in our house was new and fresh. Whereas our meal choices hardly ever repeated themselves, they ate the same dishes year after year. I was too young to understand the significance of their traditions. It seemed to me that I had come to see the exotic and found the predictable. I was the exotic one, who lived across the ocean in a place where it never rained and yet flowers grew, where the seasons hardly existed, and where my parents were creating their own traditions.

I have gone back to Italy many times since then. I have seen it through more mature eyes. I have tried to see it through my parents' eyes. My relatives' lives have not changed much since I first met them. A few years ago, a young cousin married someone from Rome. Her mother cried throughout the wedding, because her daughter was moving so far away. When I tried to console her by telling her to think how much closer her daughter would be than my parents had been to their families, she answered, "Your parents became different people from us, and look what happened. They lost you, too."

We embody very different things for each other. I go back to establish a link to my past, to see if I can catch a thread of the many reasons that made it possible for my parents to leave this world, so secure and so rooted in tradition. Slowly I learn the family secrets. Living in America, where most people are open about their pasts, I find it hard to believe that I learned only two years ago that my father had a younger brother who committed suicide. The cousin who told me this asked me to keep it to myself. "It is embarrassing for the family, especially the older ones. They must be respected," she said. I felt so sad to know that in some ways I was a stranger to my own family, who had kept a secret from me so carefully. I had learned in America to accept suicide, but here in my parents' country, people treated suicide with the same darkness as they did in Peru.

I now understand that I can't change my family. I find the old house where nothing changes, I eat porcini mushrooms in the fall, and I respect my cousins' silence when I tell them I have been divorced twice. They watch my family from a distance and discuss us with their friends whose relatives have also emigrated. We all know when to stop trying to understand.

18
MACHU PICCHU

MY FIRST VISIT to Machu Picchu and the Peruvian Andes did not take place until I was eighteen years old. The trip required many preparations, and still nothing could have readied me for what I experienced. Getting there was an adventure in itself. For several days we got up very early and drove to the airport, only to return home a few hours later because of the weather conditions. Finally one morning we took off. Our plane was small, a DC-4. Sitting on the runway, it appeared too vulnerable a vessel to carry us across the majestic Andes far to the east. For the first half-hour of our flight the plane circled in the air, trying to gain enough altitude to rise above the mountains. I sat between a young nun, who invited me to join her in praying the rosary for a safe journey, and a businessman, who, shaking his head with a dark look on his face, whispered into my ear that it was *salado*, bad luck, to have a nun on board.

The pilot announced that we had reached the proper altitude and were ready to "make the crossing." He asked us to keep our seatbelts tight and breathe through our oxygen masks. Suddenly the plane began to bounce in the air like a cocktail shaker. The nun began to pray out loud, and the businessman began to laugh hysterically. The stewardess tried to soothe him, but after a while not even she could provide comfort, because the plane shook so much.

From the windows I could see the Andes on both sides. We were flying through a corridor between two mountains, so narrow that at moments the wings seemed to touch them. When we landed at Cuzco airport, everyone clapped and the triumphant pilot announced that it had been a miraculous journey. "We fought the enemy winds and conquered them," he said proudly. The businessman told me in a voice loud enough for the nun to hear, "If they didn't let nuns fly, there wouldn't be enemy winds. Let them stay in their convents and have their fights with the devil there." The nun gave him a compassionate look.

The airport was deserted. We were the only plane that had made the crossing that day. As we gathered our luggage, a crowd of taxi drivers and tourist guides offering their services formed around us. The businessman introduced us to a friend, and after we agreed on a price for the ride to the city, we got into his taxi. The altitude made it hard to move. Our young bodies felt heavy, and we were out of breath. The taxi driver suggested that we have a *maté de coca*, an infusion made of coca leaves. We drank it suspiciously, but it soon helped us adjust.

The single-lane road that led to Cuzco was like many we were to drive on during this journey, lonely roads where the somnolent traffic was often interrupted by crossing herds of animals, mostly llamas and alpacas and their wild cousins, vicuñas and guanacos. We occasionally passed buildings made of adobe with red tile roofs. Indian women sat outside, knitting in the sun while they peddled vegetables and dried herbs. Their faces looked like a succession of variations on Saturnina's face, oval, dark, enigmatic. They were dressed in brightly colored skirts made of light wool. Multicolored ponchos were wrapped around their backs and held their babies, who surveyed the scene. Black felt hats in elegant shapes sat atop their heads. From inside the buildings we could hear Indian music, its sad monotony as desolate as the landscape.

The land around Cuzco is what the Peruvians call the *altiplano*, flat and empty, with an occasional lonely tree or cultivated with grain or potato crops. Cuzco, the Indian metropolis of Peru, is a conglomeration of red tile roofs with a seemingly infinite number of church domes soaring above them. Its narrow cobblestone streets are framed by buildings that reflect a mélange of architecture from many centuries. The lower walls are made of exquisitely shaped, massive stones of the Inca period, so finely crafted that there is no mortar between them. Above them sit the roughly cut stones of the colonial period, held together by adobe mortar. Fanciful colonial wooden balconies abound. When I first visited, Cuzco was an active city with a lazy tempo, and its inhabitants went about their daily lives unperturbed by the tourists' cameras. The natives still sported their own colorful clothing; blue jeans and T-shirts were nowhere in sight.

The Hotel de Turistas, a plain, functional building at the center of the city, was where all tourists stayed. Before terrorism scared visitors away, the hotel was always filled to capacity. A crowd of guides, who introduced themselves as "university professors" and claimed to speak several languages, crowded the entrance.

We picked a guide, who turned out to be much like the others. He was a sullen young man who called himself Yupanqui, after one of the Incas, and who read

Marx and Lenin fervently. To him, the Spanish *conquistadores* were an earlier version of the foreign capitalists on whom he blamed every social ill. He was very angry and spoke nonstop. He lost no time in telling me that Italians like my parents had raped Peru, that rich Peruvians had done the same, that the noble Indian blood would wake up one day and by violence restore Indian rule. He was no different, I think, from the the kind of Peruvians who later became members of the Shining Path: people who, possessed by their anger and intense loyalty to their cultural past, fed by their reading of communist doctrines, and made desperate by the dismal economic situation of the country, ended up creating pointless violence, which has hurt Peru very much and killed so many.

At moments Yupanqui became sentimental, especially after he had a pisco sour, and spoke of the noble Indian past, but when he realized that we knew our history well, he stopped. Then, as now, I knew that there was no use arguing. He knew how to get us where we wanted to go. We closed our ears and followed him.

Cuzco was and still is a veritable repository of treasures. Its many colonial churches, built in a high Baroque style called *churrigueresco*, stand in stark contrast to the otherwise modest buildings that make up the city. The façades, carved out of local stone, are like lace designs, partly abstract, partly reproductions of colonial signs of power such as emblems and coats of arms.

Their interiors, with altars made of gold and silver encrusted with mirrors, are a profusion of ornaments that shimmer with splendor in the daylight. Paintings of Madonnas and saints dressed in fanciful garments, their gentle expressions devoid of any sense of the brutal colonization of Peru, cover the walls. Dark carved wooden pulpits and confessionals, resplendent with detail, are places from which the religious colonization of Peru was preached and where the bewildered natives were forced to confess their "sins" to the Spanish prelates.

Our guide regaled us with stories of Spanish abuses. "The only real Spanish Catholics were two Jesuit priests who defended the Indians. The others preached that Indians were animals because they had not been baptized. Think of that! What imagination they had to further their exploitation!" At other times he claimed, "The Spaniards were too stupid and ignorant to appreciate the Inca civilization. Wait until you see Machu Picchu. It will be obvious just how stupid they were."

One day, at four in the morning, we boarded the train for our pilgrimage to Machu Picchu. The tiny engine climbed steep terrain on rails that had been laid zigzag to alleviate the difficulty of the ascent. We stopped in many small villages where the train represented the people's only contact with the outside world. At each stop, Indian women boarded the train and offered their crafts for sale.

Until recently, when the Indians began to use ar-
tificial dyes and knitting machines, Peruvian textiles were
objects of intricate beauty, whose designs and crafts-
manship had been passed from generation to generation. Before television and before terrorism, most of
the Indians accepted their bleak lives with resignation.
Then, they asked tourists to be photographed; now,
they charge to pose. For security reasons, the train
carrying the tourists no longer stops in these villages.

As the journey continued, we entered the Amazon
region, and the landscape began to change dramati-
cally. Uncontrollable, opulent masses of green vegeta-
tion surrounded us. In the distance appeared the twin
mountain peaks of Machu Picchu and Huayna Picchu.
They rise out of the Amazonian jungle, proud and
straight, as if they aspire to touch the sky. It is a sight
so overwhelmingly splendid that it is almost peerless.

Perilously built, clinging to a narrow ridge between
the two peaks, is the ancient Inca city-fortress of Machu
Picchu. It is so difficult to imagine how it was built
that it seems almost an extraterrestrial apparition. Now
buses climb up to it, but on my first visit we ascended
by mule on a narrow path at the edge of a cliff. Machu
Picchu is so magnificent that it was easy to ignore the
depth of the ravine below and be mesmerized by the
gigantic fortress that we laboriously approached.

Machu Picchu is among the many things the Indians
hid from the Spaniards. It was not until 1911 that the

American adventurer and archeologist Hiram Bingham stumbled upon it. This city of houses and ceremonial buildings was built in tiers on the lower part of the slope of a steep hill. The city was surrounded by farming terraces linked by steps and irrigated with intricate aqueducts.

When the day tourists left, those of us who had been lucky enough to get a room in the small pension on the site were left with the place all to ourselves. I wandered on, allowing myself to get lost in the hollow chambers, my mind racing through the many Incan legends I had heard throughout my life. This was a fortress and a temple built to guard an empire that extended from northern Venezuela to Patagonia, an empire with military dictators who claimed the divine right to govern, to murder rivals, to promote inequalities similar to those that exist today, an empire in which the few perpetrated poverty on the masses. This kind of fortress was built to intimidate the rulers' own people as much as their enemies.

As my mind traveled among these thoughts, I heard the distant sound of the quena, an ancient Peruvian instrument made of bamboo. I followed the music to a young Indian boy sitting at the edge of the ravine, his small herd of llamas in the background. In the dusk, against the vast emptiness of the precipice, with Huayna Picchu in the background, they cut an amazing image. The llama is an animal that by the sheer force of its beauty and elegance has gone from being the livelihood of a boy as poor as this one to being the pet of some of the richest households in Beverly Hills. The boy, his strong, sharp features contrasting with his slight body, played the simple laments of his native music. I sat listening to him until it was dark.

When I got ready to leave, he followed me. Shortly before we arrived at the pension, he asked me if I was American. I answered that I was Peruvian.

"Peruvian?" he repeated, giving me an incredulous look. Then he quickly added, "For Peruvians, my music is free."

Early the next morning, when I got up to see the sun rise between the mountains, I heard the boy's music again. He was a small boy whose ancestors had believed they ruled by divine right and who had built an intricate, powerful civilization, only to abandon it enigmatically at the arrival of the conquistadors. He contemplated a future that could only reflect the sadness of his music.

19
ENGLAND

AT FIRST London did not seem unfamiliar — not that I had given much thought to imagining it. In the early morning it appeared as gray as Lima, the fog thicker than the *neblina*. I had flown such long hours and landed at so many airports that I was tired and the grayness felt comfortable. This, I had figured out, would be my year in purgatory, my mandatory "finishing school." My plan was that it would buy me four years at an American college. I had not figured out how, but at the age of fifteen, I believed that all dreams come true.

It did not take long to realize how different everything really was. We seemed to move in a noiseless world where everyone whispered and the cars moved silently. Except for the red buses and the very green lawns, the city had a solemn, dark tone. Our hotel was so quiet that I tiptoed, and as I did, the butlers dressed in tails murmured, "Good morning, young lady." My room was an explosion of chintz, with large stuffed chairs and warm towels in the bathroom. We dined with some of my father's business associates in a restaurant that served game. Tiny pieces of lead popped out as we tried to eat the tough meat. The food was tasteless. We spent a morning at Harrods department store, where Mother bought me numerous school uniforms, all seemingly designed to make me look shapeless. At Covent Garden we saw a ballet, the dancers flying as if they were weightless. I imagined myself in my uniform and felt very sorry for myself.

Early one morning we packed ourselves into a taxi and drove off to my school. I don't remember saying goodbye to my parents; I only remember the taxi becoming a small black dot in the distance and the feeling of being very alone. I did not speak a word of English, and someone had made a mistake: I had arrived a day early. At noon, I sat alone in the empty dining room. A young nun brought me a piece of meat floating in thick brown juice. Next to the meat rested a potato and a few old-looking vegetables that I later learned were called Brussels sprouts. Hoping for a more appetizing main course, I barely touched my appetizer, only to learn that the first plate of food was the whole meal. (The next day I watched as a hundred other Latinas made the same mistake.) Dessert followed: rice dotted with an occasional raisin and cooked in something vaguely sweet, much like the baby food in jars that I would later feed to my children in America. I consoled myself by walking in the rain, which fell that whole first day, and watching my reflection in the miniature lakes that formed on the pavement.

At fifteen, I was the youngest of about a hundred bored, restless, dreamy women, most of whom were seventeen, stuck in a convent school outside London. At the time I admired us for putting up with the Englishness of it all. Now I admire the poor nuns for putting up with us. They tried everything to get us to learn English. Not much worked. We complained in Spanish while we let them drag us to the Old Vic, Covent Garden, and the Tate.

My experience in London reminded me of the Hotel

Bolívar. We girls spent most of our time inventing stories to impress each other while waiting for real life to begin. Our constant preoccupation was thinking up ways to make the nuns' lives miserable. One Sunday morning we wore the reddest of lipsticks to Mass and kissed the priest's fingers as he gave us communion. The poor priest became so agitated that he dropped the chalice. Once we locked a nun we knew to be lesbian into a room with her younger nun friend. The punishments were as childish as the misbehavior. We were almost happy to be forbidden to take a shower, since the water was so cold, or to go to a play we would not understand anyway. Our maneuvers were innocent, adolescent rebellions performed by young women preparing for a future that depended entirely on the kind of husbands they would land.

The highlight of our year was meant to be our Easter vacation trip to Ireland. We were taken around the island by bus for two weeks. It rained during our entire stay. The nuns, happy to get rid of us, left us with a chaperone, a middle-aged woman named Miss Perkins. She was joined by a young Irish guide named Patrick. Patrick was short and stocky but had a pair of very blue, romantic eyes. To keep us happy in the bus, he sang Irish songs. We all developed a crush on him and made him sing Irish lyrics over and over.

Our biggest thrill came when we discovered Irish coffee. Miss Perkins had no idea (or perhaps she pretended not to) that it was loaded with whisky. Patrick made a rule that we could only have it in bed. He happily sent us to bed early, knowing that we would get a little drunk, so that he could rest and get ready for another day of balladeering. In those days, we were so involved in our daydreams that the Irish landscape was an invisible stage for our emotional lives. Not long ago I found a picture of Patrick surrounded by a bunch of us. This photo is the only visual memento of my two weeks in Ireland.

After the school year was over, I was extremely happy to go back home and see my blue desert sky and eat Mother's cooking. I panicked, though, when I saw the gringo Cooper. I was very grateful that he did not tell my parents that I spoke almost no English.

20
HOW I GOT TO COLLEGE

AFTER MY SCHOOL YEAR in London and a trip through Europe with my parents, I returned home with only one thought in mind: to go to college in the United States. During the trip I had brought up the topic several times, with no success. My parents did not want to hear of it. They had purchased an apartment in Lima, and we were going to spend a lot of time there. Mother bought me lots of elegant clothes, and I was officially in the market for a husband. I was seventeen years old, and I wanted something different for myself.

The idea of college, which was first planted in my mind by reading Mother's magazines, had fallen on fertile ground at school in England. There, toward the end of the school year, a college student from New York had come to stay while she researched a paper. She was a tall, beautiful blonde who wore a fraternity pin. She was given a room close to mine, and we became friends. Her father had been the American ambassador to Colombia. She had lived there for a few years and had nothing but contempt for the women of my class. Her name was Cassandra Reynolds, and without knowing it, she changed my life. I wish I had kept track of her so that I could tell her so. Her life in college sounded like the life I had been born for. I made up my mind that somehow I would get there. The nebulous idea of four years in an American college became my life's obsession.

One morning I announced that I was going on a hunger strike to protest my parents' rejection of my college plans. Father gave me a look of compassion, and on Mother's face I spotted an incredulous smile. Hoping to be taken more seriously, I announced my intention to Señorita Luisa, who simply told me to grow up and not to force the will of my parents. Saturnina thought it was funny that with so many hungry people, I should choose to be hungry too.

My strike went on for a week. My stomach growled constantly, and I felt a bit dizzy. The first few days I sat at the table with everyone else and refused to eat. My brother and sister, who sympathized with my plea, gave me looks of encouragement. My parents said nothing. Toward the end of the week, I decided it would be more dramatic to stay in my room. Saturnina offered to sneak me food, but after the episode with Manuel's letter, my trust in her was limited. I just lay in bed staring at the white ceiling and feeling sorry for myself. In the distance I could hear the household noises. In my self-pity, I felt I was not even missed.

One morning as I lay in bed thinking that I was going to be left to starve myself to death, I was called into the study. Both my parents were there. Mother looked as if she had been crying, and for the first time Father seemed old to me. The morning light made his hair look white, and he bent forward as if he were tired. I was overcome by sadness. My knees trembled and my head hurt.

When it came to this sort of matter, it was usually Mother who did the talking. This time Father spoke. "Your mother and I have given a lot of thought to your desire to go to college. We wish you had not gone to this extreme to prove how serious you are. I, more than your Mother, feel that it is not what I wish for you. At your age, a young woman should be with her family, perhaps thinking about starting a family of her own with people of her own kind. But you are an intelligent, determined young woman, and times are changing, so we have decided to let you go for a year."

I was overcome by an intense desire to run and hug my parents. I loved them so much. Instead, I stood still as tears streamed down my face. Mother got up and hugged me. Finally Father said firmly, "Let us put some food in her stomach, and tomorrow we will continue this conversation."

The days that followed were agitated ones. It was the end of August and college started in September, so we had to move fast. An American Jesuit priest who had come to Tacna to start a boys' school was called by my parents to help. I did not know him very well, but my parents liked him, and he was a fervent believer in the education of women. Father laid down the rules. It had to be a Catholic school, and I had to study something useful, like accounting or economics. I wanted to be an architect, but Father did not consider that a suitable profession, and the school could not be in New York, a place he considered evil.

We soon discovered that there were not many choices. With three exceptions, Catholic colleges offered women majors only in fields such as nursing, home economics, and liberal arts. The exceptions were three Jesuit schools: Marquette, Saint Louis, and Fordham. Fordham was in New York and therefore out of the question. Mother and I looked up the other two on a map. We decided that Saint Louis was closer to Peru. When I think of the interminable visits to colleges, the tests, and the interviews my children went through before settling on what they hoped was the most suitable college for themselves, I realize just how odd our decision-making process was.

I applied to Saint Louis University sight unseen and was admitted by telegram. Mother and I packed my bags, and a week later I was on my way. The day before I left, we were sitting in the living room listening to the radio when the news came that Fidel Castro was traveling to New York. Shaking his head as he did to express displeasure, Father said, "Fidel is a communist. The Americans are going to find out when it is too late. All of Latin America is going to go communist." Looking at me, he gently added, "It is a good thing you will have a profession." I still don't know what he meant by that. I like to think it was Father's way of telling me that somewhere deep inside he approved of my decision.

21

AMERICA

THE TAXI dropped me off in front of the dormitory, a tall, anonymous building in the middle of Saint Louis. The lobby vibrated with activity. Parents and younger siblings watched as women my age dressed in blue jeans greeted one another with hysterical enthusiasm. I mustered my courage and walked to a table where a sign said REGISTRATION. An efficient-looking woman introduced herself as the dean. As she spoke, I could feel her gaze fixed on my outfit. I was wearing a green Nina Ricci suit Mother had bought for me in Europe. It was my favorite suit; it made me feel chic and modern, yet at that particular moment all I wished for was a pair of jeans.

The dean asked me my name and then searched for it on a long list. "You are not on the list," she announced, and added, "Perhaps you are in the wrong place. With an outfit like that, your parents should have sent you to a fine Eastern school." I tried hard to swallow my tears, but they got the better of me. When she realized how upset I was, she changed her attitude and in a condescending voice said, "Well, let me look again." Minutes later we figured out that she was looking in the wrong place. My name on the registration card was Gabriella Brignole. In Peru, as in other Latin countries, the mother's surname follows that of the father for formal procedures. Otherwise we use the father's. I had always been called Gabriella De Ferrari. The dean apologized for the mistake and told me that I had to "learn many new ways" and that it was "going to be hard to be so different." "You are lucky," she added. "Your roommate is a nice young woman from Tulsa, as American as apple pie. Just watch her and do as she does. You'll be all right." With that encouragement, I quickly made my way through the noisy corridors to my room. I had one thought in mind: to change before anyone saw me in my green suit.

When I arrived at my room, Lucy, my roommate, was already there. She was sitting on her bed, crying from homesickness. When she saw me, she pulled a wad of tissues from a box and dried her tears. I introduced myself. When I tried to shake her hand, the way I had been taught, Lucy let out a loud, warm laugh. "Don't ever do that here," she said. "Just say hi."

Lucy figured out quickly that I needed help. She made me into her project. We unpacked my suitcases and she told me to hide the outfits she deemed inappropriate, which was practically everything I owned, the result of endless shopping trips and many arguments with Mother. She lent me a pair of jeans, and off we went to our first meal.

Lucy took me around the cafeteria, introducing me

as "Gabriella from Peru." The reaction her introduction elicited made me feel as if I were some kind of an odd specimen. A few of the students asked, "Peru, Ohio?" It turned out that not only was I the only foreign student, but most of the girls had never before met someone from another country. I had to answer the same questions a hundred times over. I grew exhausted from telling people that we spoke Spanish in Peru, that we did not wear native costumes, and that, yes, I had eaten a hamburger before. When I got to bed, I fell asleep before I had time to review my misery. However, I remember Lucy talking to her mother on the phone and telling her about my fancy clothes from Paris and how I had never had chewing gum, and how she was going to turn me into an American and bring me home for Thanksgiving.

Lucy was a tall, large girl who attacked every task in life with immeasurable enthusiasm. She was a year ahead of me, and she knew everyone on campus. She had been to Mexico, to a border town called Tijuana. Because of that she thought herself some kind of Latino expert, and every time I did something that struck her as different, she pronounced me "just like those people in Tijuana." It drove me crazy, particularly because we Peruvians thought of ourselves as better educated than Mexicans. Besides, at that stage of my life I hadn't decided yet whether I preferred to be called Peruvian or Italian. I learned to forgive Lucy, though, because she was the kindest person I had ever met.

Lucy was an adopted child. I had never met anyone who had been adopted, because adoption was rare in Peru, and at first I assumed that adoption was something secretive and sad. But Lucy talked about it as if it were quite normal. Her mother, the first woman surgeon in Tulsa, had married when she was too old to have a child. She had found Lucy through an agency. Lucy's biological mother had gotten pregnant at fourteen and the father had refused to marry her, so she gave up Lucy for adoption. I explained to my mother that Lucy's original parents and her new mother and father had signed many papers, which made Lucy into a real daughter with the name of the adopted parents. My mother told me that adoption was a strange American custom.

On my first day of class, I was left on my own. I had to go over the name problem with every professor. I thought I had managed to get through the day just fine, but when I returned to my room, I found Lucy in a very agitated state. "Give me those cards," she ordered. "I can't believe what you did. The whole school is laughing at you." I had handed one of my calling cards to a young man who sat next to me in class. It turned out that he had spread a rumor about this foreign woman who gave away her phone number on printed cards. "It's like advertising yourself," said Lucy. From then on she was a lot stricter about what I took with me when I went out.

At times it felt as if Lucy were the reincarnation of

my mother; at other times she seemed to be my salvation. She had endless patience. She taught me American manners, to dance the jitterbug, to wear penny loafers, and to act properly American on dates. She wanted to turn me into what she called a "normal American." Her favorite thing, however, was when I read her my letters from home. She always told me how exotic it was, and how she was going to get a part-time job to save enough money to visit me in Peru.

College life turned out to be quite close to what I had expected. Soon I got used to being a bit of a curiosity, and with Lucy's encouragement I even made up a few stories about life at home. The girls had odd ideas about Latin men; they thought they were great lovers. There I was, my only experience with love being my abbreviated infatuation with Manuel, considered an expert on Latin men.

When I realized that this kind of expertise made it difficult for anyone to ask me on a date, I invented other kinds of stories. Everything I said spread through the dorm like wildfire. Even my English teacher, a cranky old priest, had heard of my tales, and he asked me to put them in writing. So it turned out that my introduction to life in America, my dreamland, also introduced my classmates to what became their dreamland. I learned that everything was relative — that a beautiful green suit could be an instrument of torture, that you could have parents who weren't really yours, and that simple calling cards were problematic. I also discovered that coming from Peru was very exotic indeed.

Lucy has remained my friend throughout the years. For her twenty-first birthday, Mother gave her a pair of pearl earrings. That night, with a hot needle and a piece of cork, I pierced her ears. When her mother saw her pierced ears during her next visit to Saint Louis, she just smiled and told me not to do it again. "In the United States," she explained, "that is a surgical procedure." Aside from mentioning matters of hygiene, Lucy's mother was trying to protect me from the criticism my act provoked, including the accusation from a fellow student that I was a savage for piercing holes in people's bodies.

When my mother died, Lucy wrote me a letter: "This morning as I was putting on my makeup I looked in the mirror. I was wearing the pearl earrings your mother gave me and I thought, 'Gabriella's mother was right. Pearls do light up the face.' The mind is a funny thing, but whenever I wear my earrings I think of your mother, and I will for the rest of my life. So that is not exactly immortality, but it's close enough." Mother would have liked to be remembered that way in Saint Louis, which was no longer just a place we chose from a map.

22

A NEW ENGLAND EPISODE

EXCEPT FOR Helen, a close relative of my husband's, I knew no one at the funeral. We had just crossed the long green lawn that led to the small church. It was a warm spring morning, and the white steeple stood tall above the yellow forsythia and the tender green leaves of the maple trees. People made their way silently. The sound of the organ could be heard in the distance. When we got there, the chapel was completely filled. We stood in the back. I had been married for only a few weeks, and this was my first American memorial service.

By marriage I had joined a proper New England family, and I was quickly realizing how isolated from reality my student life had been. From the smaller things of life to the important ones, I was learning new ways of behavior. I was told not to use my hands so much when I talked, never to hold hands with my husband in public, and not to wear patent leather shoes after Labor Day. I had been instructed in the etiquette of the thank-you note and had spent endless hours writing elaborate notes to people I did not know for gifts I had chosen myself from a bridal register.

On this particular morning, I dressed in black for

the service, only to be told that there was no need for those who were not members of the family to dress so mournfully. Helen was dressed in a neutral shade of gray. We were attending the funeral of a family friend. Helen described him as "a true Bostonian — Exeter, Harvard, and Harvard Law." She said this, as she often did, as if there were no other places to come from and no other schools to go to.

When the organ stopped and after the minister said the prayers, a succession of speeches began. Laudatory comments about the departed gentleman were delivered in muted, controlled voices. From where I stood I could see his family, serene and unflappable. I began to think of the funerals I had attended at home: the atmosphere charged with flowing emotions, everyone dressed in black, no speeches — just the time to meditate and share the loss. Here I was surrounded by what felt like a group of lead soldiers.

A young man, who must have been the dead man's son, began to talk. He also mentioned Harvard, Exeter, and Boston. I realized that I was probably the only one there who had no personal history with any of these places. I was overcome with an urge to cry, which I could not contain. My sobs were not muted. People began to turn and look discreetly in my direction. Suddenly Helen grabbed me by the arm and led me outside the chapel. "You did not even know him," she said. As we reached the lawn she added, "This is awfully embarrassing." She pointed to a cab and told me to go home. As the car started to move, she waved to us to stop. I rolled down the window to hear her say in a flutter of condescension, "Now, calm yourself, dear. For someone from your background, I know, it is a difficult thing to do, but you must learn to exercise control."

On the way home, my crying took on another dimension. I was crying because I was furious, because I knew I would never learn to control myself, and because I felt estranged. The taxi driver tried to help me and uttered something to the effect that it must be hard to lose a loved one. "I did not even know this man," I responded. He turned around and gave me a compassionate look. Happily, I have yet to learn Helen's kind of control.

23

MY FIRST BABY

THE SPRING SUN gave the room a gentle light. My mother and I sat by the crib and admired my first baby. He had come home that day, the most splendid of all April days. The house was very still. Softly, Mother began to sing one of the songs she used to sing for us on the way to the beach. The moment was only about serenity: Mother's soothing voice, my baby's scent, his tiny body wrapped in a blanket Señorita Luisa had knitted.

Just then the phone rang. It was a friend offering her congratulations. During the conversation, she asked me what language 1 spoke to my child. When I answered "Spanish," she casually replied, "What is that going to do for him when he goes to school?" Unintentionally, she started a storm of panic. I realized that I would have to make many, many decisions involving my tiny baby's life. I returned to the room, and suddenly Mother's singing took on a different dimension. It became exasperatingly confusing, almost strange. The serenity was gone. I looked out the window. There were no palm or olive trees, just maples and oaks. Mother's music seemed not to belong here.

That night, as my baby slept peacefully, trusting the world, I had strange dreams. I dreamed I was talking to him and he was screaming at me because he could not hear me. No words were coming out of my mouth. In the dream, my husband and his relatives arrived to take the baby from me. I also dreamed that my parents wouldn't speak to me anymore because they couldn't talk to their grandchild.

By the time my first child was born, I had lived in Boston for more than three years and I had learned to think of it as home. Yet the anxiety I was going through was worse than what I had felt that first day in Saint Louis in my green suit, when my name was absent from the list of students.

I embarked on endless consultations. I talked to pediatricians, psychologists, and teachers. I heard various opinions. One person told me that being bilingual caused stuttering, another that it reduced the ability to have a complete English vocabulary. Everyone agreed that the risks outweighed the opportunities. In New England at the time, the consensus was that bilingualism could hurt one's chances of doing well in the competitive school system — a system that, in the world I moved in, seemed to have as its goal attendance at an Ivy League college. I made up my mind to speak English to my baby. Yet each time, after a few words, I reverted to Spanish. No matter how determined I was, I just couldn't do it.

In my solemn efforts to be a competent mother, I had not asked my own mother's advice. One morning as I drove her to the airport to see her off to Peru, I confided my troubles to her. "I spoke to you in Italian," she said. "I had no psychologists to consult, and I don't see that you turned out any worse than your American friends." I realized that I had forgotten the most important lesson my parents had taught me: to respect my own instincts.

24

A LIMA MOMENT IN 1992

MY FRIEND AND I drove amid the jumble of cars through the noisy streets of Lima. There had been another terrorist attack and the electrical towers had burned, so the streetlights weren't working. My friend drove through the intersections, ignoring the dizzying conglomeration of vehicles attempting to do the same. The traffic police, who were supposed to compensate for the failed lights, had given up. They stood and watched the spectacle unfold. I closed my eyes, hoping we would avoid disaster.

When we got to our destination, it took us a good twenty minutes to find a parking spot. The weather was hot, but we had to keep the windows closed against the peddlers who besieged us, offering the supplies — carbon paper and tape — we would need to carry out our transaction. A heavyset middle-aged man, his baggy pants held up by wide suspenders, emerged from the crowd. As he approached us, he announced proudly, "I could tell you were the Americana." He introduced himself as Señor Morales, our facilitator, ready to lead us "through the jungle of Peruvian paperwork." We were here to take care of a routine legal matter, changing my married name to my maiden one.

The police at the door recognized Señor Morales and let us in before the crowd. A woman screamed, "How about me? I am not white enough?" No one paid any attention. We followed the facilitator through a maze of corridors filled with cardboard boxes and desks. Just as we reached our destination, an avalanche of people surged into the halls. "Don't worry," Señor Morales told me. "It is my job to get you out of here in a minute." I noticed that the building was clearly unfinished. There were no railings in the stairwell, the walls were not painted, and most of the windows were missing glass. Señor Morales explained that this was the temporary headquarters for the courthouse. The new one was still being built. A woman standing nearby said loudly, "Of course, in the year 3000." My friend told me that this building had been condemned: the speculators had built four more floors than the foundation could support.

I was overwhelmed by the number of people who were filtering in, all wearing looks of patience, as if they were used to waiting all their lives. I thought of my friends in America, who despair at the long lines at the Registry of Motor Vehicles. I noticed that there were other people like Señor Morales, accompanied by people like us, who could afford to hire them. "You are about to enjoy the War of the Facilitators," my friend told me, "but don't worry, Morales is an old pro."

A young man in a blue polyester suit arrived. His

comb had left heavy paths in his oily black hair. The facilitators followed him to a small desk in front of an office door. "Morales," he yelled in a commanding voice. Morales gave me a look of satisfaction and ran to the desk while all the others booed. A new dynamic set in. Beneath a sign that read "Under penalty of jail, no bribery is to take place on these premises," Morales and the clerk discussed the cost of this transaction. They talked as if no one were listening. When they reached an agreement, a man who was standing next to us handed me a card. "Morales is very expensive," he said. "Next time, use me. It would be an honor to be of service to such a distinguished lady."

My friend, who sensed my apprehension, reassured me. "We are not doing anything illegal. We are just getting it done fast." I knew this was not something that could get me into trouble, but I wondered about the people who could not afford a facilitator and who returned day after day to wait in line. Most didn't seem to mind; they were used to this process. Morales asked me for a certain sum, preferably in dollars. I was not used to this, and I became extremely anxious. "What if we get caught?" I asked my friend. "You have lived in the United States too long," he replied.

The judge's assistant then ordered someone who was sitting at a small desk across the hallway to give him the typewriter. A small scene developed when another facilitator demanded that whatever was being typed should be finished first. We waited. The typewriter must have been at least thirty years old, and the ribbon barely made a mark. When our turn arrived, the facilitator provided paper, carbon paper, and an eraser. "Next time," he told the clerk jokingly, "I'll bring you a ribbon for the machine."

"Phenomenal," said the clerk. "This ribbon is driving us crazy. We ordered one a month ago and it has not come."

The outspoken woman commented again. "Don't bring him anything. He'll sell it to pay his mistress." Everyone laughed.

The clerk excused himself. As he disappeared, he said, "I'll be gone for just a moment. I think the judge has arrived." The facilitator tried to engage me in the kind of conversation I dread. He wanted to know how long it would take for this kind of thing to be completed in America. I knew he imagined a country of breathtaking efficiency. "It's slow there, too," I told him. He didn't believe me. I switched the topic. I felt better not destroying his illusions about America.

Finally the clerk returned and beckoned to Morales. There was a long, loud exchange. My friend told me to be prepared: the judge probably wanted more money. Morales, looking very dejected, embarked on what could have become a long explanation. My friend interrupted him: "Just tell us how much." As I gave Morales the money, the facilitator who had given me his card said very loudly, "I told you, he is very expensive, and besides, he is probably pocketing half of it himself. The clerk is his brother-in-law."

After a few minutes I was ushered into the judge's office to sign the papers. It was a windowless space no bigger than a large walk-in closet. The only piece of furniture was a tiny desk in the middle. The rest of the space was thickly populated by piles of papers tied with string. There was a strong smell of humidity and dust. The judge was nowhere to be seen. Morales told me the clerk could imitate his signature so that "no one can tell." The facilitator pulled out a little box, and I was fingerprinted. The papers were filled with stamps and sealed. "Very official," Morales told me. "They'll love them in New York." He then raced across the street to get the papers photocopied and left a copy on top of one of the piles, and we marched off. The crowd outside the office was the same group that had been there when we arrived, all still waiting patiently for their turn.

25
GRINGA LATINA FROM PERU

IT WAS A HOT, steamy day in Manhattan, one of those days when newscasters tell people not to go outside unnecessarily. As I listened to the weather forecast, I made my decision. It did not matter how hot it was; I would wear stockings. It was a big day for me. After almost thirty years of living in America, I was on my way to becoming an American citizen. I wanted to treat the event with the significance it had for me.

Early in the morning, I walked slowly to the courthouse, watching the streets wake up. I wanted to arrive before everyone else. On the way I bought myself a bagel. It seemed that day the appropriate American breakfast. When I reached the courthouse, a long line had already formed. A guard commanded in a loud voice, "Aliens, gather at the left of the entrance." Alien: that was the name I had been called by the immigration office all the years that I had lived in America. I pondered the meaning of this word, as I had so often. *Alien* — a word that is used to describe something strange, repugnant, adverse. It always amazed me that the immigration office had not been able to think of something more dignified.

I studied the crowd. Some people were so assimilated that it was hard to tell they were "aliens." The two hundred gathered that morning represented an extraordinary mélange of people. As different as the backgrounds were, I could detect a division. There were those like me, who had dressed up and seemed to view this moment as a solemn event, and there were those, usually younger ones dressed in T-shirts and shorts, who treated this moment in a relaxed way. To them, perhaps, nationality was simply a formality that would make their lives easier and open doors for them.

Minutes later we were ushered into a large wood-paneled room and told to wait to be called for the final review of our papers. It was the culmination of a long process of endless paperwork, a process that because of its length and tediousness had given me plenty of time for meditation. As I sat and waited for my turn, my mind reviewed the dozens of conversations I had had with myself before deciding to take this step.

I thought of my parents, who had embraced Peru and Italy with equal fervor, yet it had never occurred to them to give up their Italian citizenship. I thought of my children, who were Americans and to whom Peru and Italy were spiritual antecedents. They most probably would never be in the position to make a choice such as this. I thought about the Vietnam War and how odd it had seemed that so few of my friends felt patriotic about it; the war I had grown up hearing about had been the subject of strong Peruvian feelings. I thought about how awful it was to be called an alien every time I returned to America, the place I considered home. I smiled to myself to think how envious I had been of my friends who did jury duty, something I could not do, in spite of the fact that I paid taxes and obeyed American laws. I remembered the day a few years before when I had felt proud because I was able to tell Señorita Luisa that I was still a Peruvian. I thought of Saturnina, who never came across concepts such as nationality; to her, there was simply her kind and our kind. I recalled my classmates in Saint Louis, to whom I was the first foreigner they had met, and of my other American friends, who simply couldn't believe that I had so much anxiety about changing my nationality. I wondered if anyone else in the room had similar thoughts.

The judge came in to give us our oath. We all stood as she entered. I repeated the lines, and as I did, I looked around the room and wondered how everyone there had arrived at this ceremony. I thought of the thousands of goodbyes, the renunciations of home and friends, the journeys to America, the confused expectations of what awaited us on these new shores, the struggles to learn a new language and eat new foods. I spotted a small Asian man dressed in a three-piece suit. He must have been in his seventies. Like me, he was wiping away a tear. He was my fellow American, and yet we were completely different.

As I left the room clutching my certificate of citizenship, I came across a large Spanish-speaking family holding flowers and a bottle of champagne to celebrate their new American. I imagined them to be Peruvian, and I stopped to watch their emotional outburst. The certificate no longer mattered; neither did the nationality. I was still the same gringa Latina from Peru.

26
MOTHER'S FINAL JOURNEY

THE SHADOW of the plane flew across the flat desert. In the noon light, the dry expanse appeared to be a soft pink canvas across which a large bird moved, silent and dark, bearer of the solemn secret of death. We were carrying Mother's body with us to Tacna on its way to its final destination, near Father, in the small cemetery at the end of the long row of dusty trees. Only the roar of the engines intruded on our silence. I sat in between my brother and sister; we held one another's hands. We could not talk. We shared too much sorrow. It had all happened so fast: my brother calling me on the phone in the middle of the night, my husband and children leaving me at the airport in New York, my sister waiting for me in Miami for that interminable night flight, cut off from the world. When I saw my brother's face at the airport in Lima, I did not need to hear him say it.

At the hospital, Mother had a few hours left. She had waited for the three of us to gather. Like robots, we did the necessary things in the hours that followed.

Now, one of the gringo Cooper's planes sheltered us on a journey we did not want to take. The brilliant sunlight blinded me as I disembarked, and it was not until I reached the bottom of the steps that I realized how many people had come to be with us. I heard someone utter the name I had been called as a child, a name I stopped using when I went to boarding school. I had not been back to Tacna since Mother had left for Lima because of her illness. Even before that, my visits had been short. I had spent most of the time at home with Mother. Today at the airport there were many faces I did not recognize. For a brief moment I thought they were not talking to me. I let them hold me: familiar scents, familiar names. I was among Mother's friends, among the friends of my youth.

The crowd moved me to a car. We drove slowly through the familiar streets to the chapel of my old school. A mass was being celebrated. Mother had died the day before Easter, and the priest spoke of resurrection. I did not find comfort in his words. Solace came from the white roses that Pablo had cut and the nuns had arranged in the chapel: to me, they were a symbol of Mother, of the world she had created. Pablo gave me a few. I held them, waiting to make my final gift.

It was cool and gray by the time we left the cemetery. We dreaded returning home. I couldn't imagine being there without Mother. The house had been dusted in a rush, and there were no flowers. Saturnina came with us. She fed us dinner and then prepared to go home. I walked her to the gate, the dogs barking at my feet. I felt like a stranger in my own house.

Our terrible task was to settle the material part of Mother's life. The house had to be sold. We needed to divide the belongings that could be taken with us. We did this mostly in silence, trying to respect Mother's wishes. Sadness acted as an analgesic that soothed the pain. I still don't know how the three of us managed to perform our task.

We had lived in the house as a family for many years. The changes Mother had made were a testament to the life she had created for her years alone. I was looking not to decode that life but for reassurances that it had been a peaceful one. I was also looking for the parts of me she had chosen to keep close to her. I think my brother and sister felt the same, which is why we performed our chores silently. Each object had a mute voice that spoke to me: the telephone next to her bed, on which we had talked so often; our pictures in simple silver frames, the one of Father larger than the others, his reassuring smile and inquisitive eyes protecting us still; the tired copies of *The Divine Comedy* and other books she had read; copies of what I had written myself, next to the dictionary so that she would not miss a word in translation; the letters and photographs she had chosen to keep, which told about the parts of my life I chose to share with her; my small and big triumphs and my small and big defeats. From here in this remote part of our Peru, Mother had watched closely as I developed into my own person, and as the life she had built for me was replaced by the life I was building for myself.

In a special box we found the letters Mother and Father had written to each other, a part of Mother's life we knew little about. Had she left them there for us to read? Should we read them? As we walked through these decisions, we realized once more how much we shared as siblings: the incredible bond of our parents. We were three grownups who had already made the big choices, among them the choice of how to interpret our parents' lives. I had chosen long ago to think about theirs as lives for celebration, not for exploration. I was happy to leave large territories unexamined, to render my parents the kind of respectful privacy I felt they would have wanted from me. My decisions appeared unusual to many of my American friends, who live in a world where other people's lives are intensely explored. Although I am prepared to have my own life explored in such ways by my children, I wanted to keep my parents' lives intact.

When we left the house a few days later, it had been emptied of the things we wanted to take with us. I did not go in to see it one last time. I took a final walk through the garden. I inhaled the scents and took them with me forever. I did not turn to look back as the car drove off. I had said my goodbyes. I had answered my questions.

In the plane, this time alone, flying in the cloudless

night sky, I looked forward to returning to my own life: to my family, born and raised in America; to the tall buildings aiming at the sky; to speaking English, the language of my most complicated thoughts; to the scent of pine and sage in my garden; to the trees watered by rainclouds; to the intoxicating murmurs of New York City; to my friends, who have accepted me so unquestioningly; to being an adult; to living my life as my own version of a gringa Latina.

A GRINGA LATINA COOKING SAMPLER

During the last few years of Mother's life, I had the good fortune to be able to visit her often. We spent many gentle, quiet days together. Mother never lost her curiosity or her enthusiasm for life. Even though her energy was ebbing, she embarked on a few projects. One of them was compiling what she called her family's "cooking explorations." In the early morning, her favorite time of day, she sat at her desk and in her perfect penmanship systematically wrote out hundreds of recipes. To her own favorites she added the ones my sister and I had sent her through the years.

The recipes are the legacy of a woman who wove cooking into the fabric of her life, giving to it her very personal vocabulary. Her cooking, as her life, combined the many cultures she had encountered. Mother was just as curious to learn from Señorita Luisa the myriad ways in which generations of her family had prepared the wondrous Peruvian potato as she was to read the perfect recipe for wild pheasant and porcini mushrooms from a five-star French chef, or to listen to the shortcuts I had taught myself for preparing casseroles for my young children when I was juggling home and career.

The roots of Mother's cooking had no boundaries, and neither did the techniques. To everything she added her own touches. When she could not find saffron, she substituted turmeric or ground coriander; when there was a shortage of butter, she made her own. When she could not find cinnamon to sprinkle on her famous meringues, she used a combination of thinly shaved bitter chocolate and grated vanilla beans, which tasted much better than the cinnamon suggested in the original recipe.

The range of the recipes was enormous. There were the simple sandwiches of oil, tomato, salt, and garlic with which she used to greet us when we returned from school, and the laborious flaky pastry layered with as many as four different creams that she served for Father's birthday. There were the cold stuffed vegetables for our picnics at the beach, and her Sunday ravioli, stuffed with spinach, ricotta, and sweetbreads and topped with a lush porcini sauce. When Mother cooked, she never measured. To her, spoonfuls and half-cups were merely pinches or handfuls, and each recipe had several variations, according to what was available and in season. The recipes are those of a magician in her kitchen, performing her experimental tricks and following her intuition while her small family audience watched in admiration.

The recipes that follow are a few I have chosen as a celebration of Mother's cuisine. They encapsulate the sweet taste of my youth. They are inventive and spontaneous, a brilliant mix that reflects the sense of discovery Mother acquired during her travels. It was hard to select the recipes, since there was nothing that Mother did not try, and repetition was not a trait of her cuisine. I hope that readers who decide to try them will share the sense of adventure that they embody, for they come from the table of a passionate woman who above all loved to please and surprise her family.

I have adapted these recipes for ingredients found in the United States. Unless otherwise noted, they serve six people.

*L*OCRO

This is a recipe that Saturnina taught Mother. It is an Andean dish of humble origins and in its original version was probably made mostly of chili peppers, pota-

toes, and pumpkin. It is rich enough to make a wonderful Sunday supper by itself. We ate it during the
few cold days of winter, served with a toasted grainy
bread that we dipped into the soupy stew.

Purée enough winter squash or pumpkin to make 4
cups. Defrost a package of frozen peas. Boil 4 large
potatoes and cut them into bite-size pieces.

In a heavy soup pot, sauté 1 large, finely chopped
onion, 1 chopped clove of garlic, and 1 teaspoon of red
pepper flakes. When they are golden, add the pumpkin
purée, the peas, and the potatoes. Cook for ten minutes, stirring constantly. Add salt to taste.

Just before serving, add ¾ cup of chopped farmer's
cheese and a touch of white vinegar. If the stew is too
thick, add some milk. Serve very hot.

STEAMED FISH WITH GREEN SAUCE OR BLACK OLIVE SAUCE

This is an elegant dish that is ideal for a summer meal.
Mother served it as an appetizer. It is delicate; the trick
is not to overcook the fish, so that it retains its texture
and flavor. Mother served the fish lukewarm, to avoid too
much contrast with the cold sauce. She accompanied

the dish with a salad of green beans and tomatoes and with warm boiled baby potatoes sprinkled with parsley.

The green sauce is based on a traditional Italian recipe. The black olive sauce was Mother's tribute to the lush black olives of the Tacna Valley, but Greek olives also work well. It is richer than the green sauce, and it is ideal for dark fish such as bluefish and tuna.

GREEN SAUCE: In an electric blender, mix ¾ cup of virgin olive oil, a large bunch of broadleaf parsley, 2 cloves of garlic, and salt to taste. In a separate bowl, soak 3 slices of chopped white bread in just enough white vinegar to make the bread soft. When the bread is soft, add the blended mixture. Add 3 tablespoons of capers and 2 finely chopped hard-boiled eggs.

BLACK OLIVE SAUCE: Pit and chop 1 pound of olives. Soak a bunch of green onions in boiling water for a few minutes, then chop enough to make 1 cup and add them to the olives. Add 1 cup of homemade mayonnaise, salt to taste, and a generous pinch of cayenne pepper. Blend in a food processor.

TO ASSEMBLE: Steam enough fish — I use sole or a similar white fish — to serve six and let it cool. Arrange it on a large platter and cover it with one of the sauces.

CORN PIE

This Peruvian version of shepherd's pie is one of Señorita Luisa's recipes and one of my favorite childhood dishes. For very special occasions, Señorita Luisa used chopped pigeon meat for the stuffing. Mother used ground beef and sometimes added chunks of cooked chicken. The dish is best when made with fresh summer corn, but frozen corn is good too. At home it was served with a hot-pepper sauce on the side.

THE CRUST: In a blender, mix 3 cups of corn kernels, 1 cup of milk, 4 tablespoons of oil, 1 tablespoon of sugar, and 1 egg. This should make a thick batter.

THE STUFFING: Sauté 1 large chopped onion and 3 chopped garlic cloves in 4 tablespoons of olive oil. Add one pound of lean ground beef and, if you like, chunks of cooked chicken. Stir in 3 large ripe tomatoes, peeled and chopped. Add chili powder and oregano to taste and a generous pinch of cinnamon. Cook for half an hour, stirring frequently.

TO ASSEMBLE: Spread half of the corn batter in a 9-by-12-inch glass baking dish. Spread the stuffing on top and cover it with 20 pitted and sliced black Greek olives and a handful of raisins. Then spread the remaining batter over the top, sprinkle it with paprika and a little oregano, and dot it with butter. (Sometimes Mother would sprinkle on a handful of pine nuts as well.) Bake for 1 hour at 350°. Serve hot.

ORTA PASQUALINA

This is one of the triumphs of Genoese cooking. It is laborious to make, but well worth the effort. As the name indicates, it is traditionally served at Easter. Mother served it for Sunday lunch during artichoke season.

THE STUFFING: Cook 12 or 14 fresh artichokes until tender. Scrape the edible parts from the leaves and chop the hearts, to make about 2 cups. Fry 1 chopped onion, 2 chopped cloves of garlic, and a pinch of oregano in 4 tablespoons of olive oil. Remove the pan from the heat and add the artichokes, 1 cup of cottage cheese, a large handful of grated Parmesan cheese, a pinch of black pepper, and 3 beaten eggs. Mix well.

TO ASSEMBLE: Line a deep round baking dish with 3 leaves of phyllo pastry, leaving enough overlapping the sides to cover the center. Spoon the artichoke mixture inside, then make 4 depressions in it and drop a raw egg into each one. Cover the mixture with the phyllo and fold the sides over the top. Paint the top with egg yolk mixed with a bit of water. Bake for 1 hour at 350°. Let cool a little, then carefully ease the torta from the dish onto a serving plate. This dish can be served cold as well as hot.

OSSO BUCCO

This is a Peruvian rendition of the traditional Italian recipe for veal shanks. Mother's idea of adding hot peppers to the original dish makes it heartier. A wonderful winter meal, it is even better served with a thick, creamy risotto. Instead of flavoring the risotto with saffron, which was difficult to find in Peru, Mother used turmeric and a bit of coriander, strong flavors that balance the pungent taste of the peppers.

In a large soup pot, sauté 6 large veal shanks in oil, taking care not to let them fall apart. When they are brown, add 1 cup of red wine, 2 large chopped tomatoes, 1 large chopped onion, a bay leaf, 2 chopped hot red peppers, a pinch of rosemary, turmeric and coriander to taste, and 2 chopped cloves of garlic. Cook for 2 hours. If the mixture becomes too dry, add a little tomato paste thinned with water. Add salt if you like at the end, so the meat retains its juices. Serve hot.

*C*IMA RIPIENA (STUFFED VEAL)

This great summer dish was one of our family's favorite foods for lunch at the beach. Mother served it cold, sliced with cold stuffed vegetables. Both dishes are of Genoese origin, but Mother added a Peruvian touch by serving them with a hot-pepper sauce.

THE STUFFING: Remove the crusts from 4 slices of white bread, chop them, and soak them in enough milk to cover. In a frying pan, sauté 1 large finely chopped onion, 2 chopped cloves of garlic, a handful of finely chopped dried porcini mushrooms, and 1 cup of lean ground veal in a little olive oil. As this mixture is cooking, add 1 cup of boiled peas. In a bowl, beat 3 or 4 eggs with a generous pinch of oregano, a large handful of grated Parmesan cheese, and the soaked bread. Add this to the sautéed meat and cook for a few minutes, seasoning to taste with salt and pepper.

TO ASSEMBLE: Stuff the pouch in a veal breast with the mixture and sew it closed with cooking twine. Place the veal in a deep pot, cover it with chicken broth, and cook it over low heat for 1½ hours. Remove it from the pot and drain it by placing it in a colander and pressing it with a weight. After it has cooled, slice and serve.

COLD STUFFED VEGETABLES

This wonderful Italian recipe is made even better by the addition of hot peppers. Although it is time-consuming to prepare, the results are truly delicious, and it can be made a day in advance.

THE CASES: Cut enough zucchinis, small eggplants, onions, tomatoes, and hot red peppers for six in half and scoop out the insides into a bowl. (Throw away the pepper seeds if you don't want this dish to be too spicy.) Parboil the vegetable cases so that they are barely tender, then set them aside to cool.

THE STUFFING: Chop the vegetables in the bowl, then mix them with 2 slices of chopped crustless white bread soaked in milk, 1 cup of grated Parmesan cheese, a large handful of chopped porcini mushrooms, a little oregano, and 1 chopped onion. Sauté this mixture in 2 tablespoons of olive oil for a few minutes. Add 3 eggs, stir briskly, and cook for a few more minutes. Season to taste.

TO ASSEMBLE: Fill the cool vegetable cases with the stuffing mixture. Line a large baking dish with several layers of very thinly sliced potatoes generously sprinkled with olive oil, finely chopped garlic, oregano, and salt. Place the stuffed vegetables on top, arranging them as close together as you can. Bake for 1 hour at 350°. Let the dish cool thoroughly before slicing and serving.

PASTA WITH PORCINI MUSHROOM SAUCE

Once a year, packages of dried porcini mushrooms would arrive from our relatives in Italy. The unusual delicate scent of the mushrooms permeated the air, embodying the many mysteries of my parents' native country. These were the porcinis of the Ligurian Riviera, which connoisseurs of gastronomic delights claim to be the best because they grow under chestnut trees. Mother used them sparingly, mostly in the stuffings that are so popular in Genoese cooking, but when they arrived each year she would indulge us with a feast of pasta topped with this extraordinary sauce of her own invention.

Wash, soak, and coarsely chop 2 cups of porcini mush-rooms, saving the water. In a blender, mix 3 large cloves of garlic with ¾ cup of virgin olive oil, 3 large tomatoes, and a pinch of salt. Place this mixture in a saucepan and cook over very low heat for 20 minutes. If the sauce is too thick, add a little of the water in which the mushrooms soaked. Add the chopped mushrooms and cook for 10 minutes more. Serve over spaghettini and top with Parmesan cheese.

$\mathscr{P}$ICANTE DE LANGOSTINOS (SPICY CRAYFISH STEW)

This dish is a Peruvian delicacy. Picante is as close to being the Peruvian national dish as ceviche is, and there are many ways of preparing it. Peruvians make it with shrimp, but Mother adapted the recipe by using crayfish, which were easier to get and tastier. Picante can also be made with chicken, rabbit, lamb, beef, duck, or pork. The meat should be cut into small pieces so it can absorb the flavor of the sauce.

Chop 3 large onions and 3 cloves of garlic. Purée 3 large hot peppers in a blender with a little water. Cook the onions, garlic, and hot-pepper mixture in 2 table-spoons of olive oil over low heat for 20 minutes. Add

2 pounds of crayfish tails and a tiny bit of boiling water to the pan. Chop 3 slices of crustless white bread and soak them in ½ cup of evaporated milk until the bread is soft, then add it to the pan. Sprinkle with oregano and a little more olive oil and cook for an additional 5 minutes. Serve on a bed of rice, garnished with chopped hard-boiled eggs and chopped celery leaves.

PAPA A LA HUANCAINA

This is one of the most popular Peruvian dishes, and therefore there are hundreds of ways of making it. Mother devised the following recipe using American ingredients during one of her visits with me. In Peru, papa a la huancaina is served as an appetizer; Mother served it as hors d'oeuvres at cocktail parties.

In a blender, mix ½ cup of peanut butter, 1 cup of cottage cheese, 1 teaspoonful of red pepper flakes, a pinch of cumin, salt to taste, and enough milk to give the sauce a velvety texture.

Boil enough tiny purple potatoes to serve 6 people. Arrange them on a tray with some toothpicks and place the sauce in the middle as a dip.

*F*IG COMPOTE

Mother served this delicious compote with her home-made vanilla ice cream. It is thick and rich, almost a meal in itself.

Bring 3 cups of water, 1 cup of honey, and ½ cup of sugar to a boil in a large saucepan. When the liquid is boiling, add 1 pound of dried figs and cook until they are soft, about 20 minutes. Remove the figs to a serving bowl. Reduce the liquid in the pan to about 1 cup by boiling it rapidly. Remove it from the heat and let it cool completely before pouring it over the figs. Garnish with grated almonds.

*F*RIED ROUND PUFFS
(for one)

Señorita Luisa made these ethereal puffs. I remember her at the stove, lifting almost weightless, perfectly round puffs from the very hot oil. She would then arrange them carefully on a large platter and top them with a heavy, dark syrup made of sugar cane (maple syrup is a good substitute).

Mix together 1 large tablespoon of flour, 1 egg yolk, 1 teaspoon of baking powder, and a teaspoon of vodka. Roll the dough into small balls and drop them into very hot vegetable oil. When they turn golden brown, lift them carefully from the oil and place them on a serving platter. Sprinkle with powdered sugar and top them with syrup. They must be served very hot.

$\mathscr{F}$RIED SWEET MILK

This Ligurian dessert is time-consuming to make and requires some skill, since you must get the texture just right and fry the dough very quickly.

In a saucepan, mix 4 eggs, 4 tablespoons of sugar, 2 tablespoons of flour, and 2 cups of milk. Bring to a slow boil and cook over low heat, stirring constantly, for half an hour. Pour the mixture onto a cool cutting board or wax paper that you have sprinkled with icewater. The dough should be about 1 inch thick.

When the mixture has cooled, cut it into oblong pieces. Mix an egg with a little water and dip each piece very carefully into it. Roll the pieces in breadcrumbs and drop them one by one into very hot vegetable oil. When they are golden brown, remove them carefully and sprinkle them with powdered sugar. Serve hot.

ZABAGLIONE
(for one)

On very special occasions, Mother would bring us zabaglione to eat in bed just before we went to sleep. Although it is usually considered a dessert for grownups, Mother made it for us children in individual portions.

Beat an egg yolk with 1 tablespoon of sugar and 1 tablespoon of Marsala until the mixture is almost green. Add a tiny bit of grated lemon peel. Cook in a double boiler until the texture is creamy. Allow to cool a little before serving.